"The Princess of Broome", exceptional necklace of 18 carats of Australian pearls measuring over 20 mm in diameter (Foundation for the Pearl, San Marino)

Jewelry Design in the 21st Century

For Sabine

MOUAWAD, *necklace of black Tahiti pearls measuring between 11 and 15 mm interspersed with gold pieces set with 16.36 carats of rubies, held in place with a clasp in yellow gold set with 1.92 carats of diamonds*

CLAUDE MAZLOUM

Jewelry Design in the 21st Century

IN COLLABORATION WITH:

Tiziana and Massimo ALOISIO

Maria-Grazia DI GIANDOMENICO

Alberto GIORGI

Mieke GOVAERTS and Tiziano ANDORNO

Randa KHALIL

Bernd MUNSTEINER

Simonne MUYLAERT-HOFMAN

Antonino RANDO

Agathe SAINT-GIRONS

Kurt and Christophe SCHAFFO

Gregor TELGMANN

Wilma VIGANÒ

Gabriele WEINMANN

GREMESE

Photography credits: Tiziana and Massimo Aloisio 70, 72, 73, 74, 75; Studio Amista 97; Vivian Paul Anton 185; Bargnesi-Budassi 114, 118; André Barsamian 25; Robert Baumann 164, 166, 167, 168, 169; Oddo Boni 117; Antonio Caetano 88 (top); Cannatello 126, 127; Anna Cella 104 (top); Won-Woo Chang 162; Paul De Backer 132, 133; De Grisogono 68, 69; Sandra De Wachtere 96; Viviane Debbas 62, 63; Bart Design 122, 123; Maria-Grazia di Giandomenico 178, 181, 182; Serge Domingie 76, 77; Dikran Duvenjian 61; Rodolfe Fafournoux 149 (bottom), 151 (bottom), Roberto Ferratini 11; Foto 2000 44, 46, 47, 48, 183; William Germani 95; Rudiger Gohr 156; Melkon Hagopian 64 (top), 65; Vincent Jaumin 98; Jos Joosen 107; Randa Khalil endpapers 186, 187; Koala Preziosi 159; Jean-Jacques L'Heritier 143; Florence Lehmann 152 (bottom); William Lempke 184; Marcello Lerner 100; Lorne Liesenfeld 12, 26, 28, 29, 30, 31, 32, 33, 35, 153 (bottom); Claudine Maddens 101; Claude Mazloum 4, 14, 24; Messe München/Loske 58 (top); Franz Miko 16-17, 18, 19, 20, 21, 22, 23; Sigrid Mittag 154; Mouawad 6, 52, 53, 54, 55; Pasquale Modica 158; Thiazo Moracs 88 (bottom); Rodrigue Najjarian 108, 109; Gabriella Noris 49; Lloyd Park 110, 111; Orlando Pastorello 60, 119; Stefan Pauli 124, 128, 129, 130, 131; Erwin Pauly 40, 41, 42, 43; Fotostudio Pejot 82, 86; Eveline Perroud 176; Pino Pianta 105; Fred Pierre-François 147, 149 (top), 150, 151 (top); Platin Gilde International 78, 155; Antoine Preziuso 177 (top); Antonio Puzzutiello 10; Marco Rabatti 76, 77; Maurizio Riccardi 56, 57, 58 (bottom), 59; Lorenzo Ricci 50, 51; Donatella Righi Fortuna 103; Roberge 171, 172, 173, 174, 175, 177 (bottom); Rolee 106; Christophe Schaffo 170; Marijke Seresia 102; Somos 94, 120, 121; Angelo Spinelli 66, 67, 112; Therese Sudre 99; Alexandra Telgmann 83; Gregor Telgmann 84, 85, 87; Fred Thomas 38, 145, 153 (top), 161, 163; Felix Tirry 134, 137, 138, 139, 141; Krista and Grety Vandevelde 90, 91, 92, 93; Jan Vanschoenwinkel 113; Daniel Virtuoso 64 (bottom), 104 (top); Alfred Watson 89; David Wheeler 36, 37; Marek Wilhelm 39, 144; Pierre Zabbal 146, 152 (top); Doron Zussman 142

Original title: Joailliers du XXIe siècle

Translation: Laura Clarke

Jacket design by: Sergio Alberini

Phototypeset and Photolitography:
Graphic Art 6 s.r.l. – Roma
E-mail: dva@uni.net

Printed and Bound by: Conti Tipocolor – Calenzano (Fi)

GREMESE
1st Edition © 1999
New Books s.r.l.
Via Virginia Agnelli, 88 – 00151 Rome
Fax +39/0665740509
E-mail: gremese@gremese.com
Website: www.gremese.com

ISBN 88-7301-310-4

SUMMARY

I

II

III

Tama Lusy

IV

Creations by Jama Lusy for "Vita"

I: *"Starry sky"*
(Cabochon sapphire and brilliants)

II: *"Heart"*
(Platinum ring, heart-shaped cabochon ruby and brilliants)

III: *"Dew"*
(Platinum ring, cabochon emerald and brilliants)

IV: *"Moonlight"*
(Platinum ring, cabochon sapphire, moonstones and diamonds)

Preface

Drops of color, source of everlasting joy...

Together with the clepsydra, jewelry has always been one of the most meaningful testimonies to an age, a social group, tendencies and customs... to culture. To an opportunity for ongoing dialogue, full of reflections. These extraordinary pages hypothesize a future humanity. The third millennium, full of magical uncertainties and ambitious hopes, all to do with relieving the problems of need and survival experienced by millions of people.

This jewel-book is a message of hope and joy. Moreover, the charm of this refined and instinctive fruit of human creativity and manual labor attests to the unending nature of joy and optimism. For this reason, the images in this book form a sort of perfect time-keeper which never stops, and which has always marked the aspiration and hope for a universe governed by harmony and eternal love, even when these qualities are hard to trace, when men seem like robots, incapable of an intense interior life. Even when the clepsydra marks time with an unpredictable material...

Princess GRAZIA DE MARCO BORGHESE

Creator of jewels
Pseudonym: Tama Lusy

Introduction

In the universe of jewelry, there are several categories of manufacturer, of which the most common are: the big names, the labels, the signatures, the artists, the artisans, the creators, and other designers. Everything combines in a fabulous crisscross which does nothing to simplify the choice for the person – male or female - who wants to look at, purchase or present a beautiful jewel.

However, we all know that there is nothing "big" about the so-called "big names" or "big labels" once their advertising budgets have been put to one side: these make even the most banal of jewels seem special in the eyes of the purchaser, whom I consider to be the victim of the professional brainwashing to which he is subjected by the numerous advertising or promotional campaigns staged by people able to afford them.

But there are also real artists who dedicate themselves entirely to the search for new materials and forms, innovative colors and techniques, and different conceptions of the specific art form that is jewelry.

This book, whose primary aim is to disclose to the public the hidden tendencies of the third millennium, has met a number of obstacles before reaching you. It has taken more than ten years of research, visits to a large number of goldsmiths throughout the world, and publicity in the professional press in order that every creator might send me his or her comments. I have had very varied replies. There is the famous Genoese artist who agrees to show me his work only if I dedicate the whole book to him, and the accredited jeweler in Place Vendôme who does not deign so much as to reply, his publicity agent having already put together a book that is exclusively his own. Some creators do not accept comparison, either because they are convinced of being the best, or because they know that their lines do not stand up in relation to others. It is the public that bears the cost of this obtuse mentality that creates a barrier between the person who wants to understand and his jeweler. However, I thankfully received numerous positive and constructive replies from all over the world. You will find a selection of unusual objects capable of transmitting messages, even feelings. These are the fruits of hard labor, in-depth research and authentic thought. Happy reading and happy choosing.

Claude Mazloum

CHAPTER I

Magic Pearls

In collaboration with GABRIELE WEINMANN

Pearls...
Gathered carefully
In the fingertips.
Combined with jewels
Resplendent with gold,
Wear them around your neck,
On your breast!
Allah's raindrops,
Ripened in their modest casket.

Goethe
The East-West Divan
Book by Suleika

Magic! There can be no better term to describe the exchange that takes place when pearls come into contact with skin fit to receive them, as if at that precise moment they take on a special brightness. It is even possible to talk of a magical incarnation if, in addition to this, the eyes sparkle and the beginnings of a smile appear, accompanied by a slight movement.

The magic of pearls triggers a play of mysterious interactions at the exact point where skin and pearls are in harmony. The skin gives the pearls the limpid shine of dewdrops. For their part, pearls can give the skin a silky tint. Or perhaps it is the pearls themselves that are transformed into silk? The rules of the game have never been established in writing; they emerge as the game progresses, and respect for the rules happens of its own accord.

Goldsmiths such as Lalique and Fabergé are said to have employed "pearl wearers", women on whose skin pearls would regain their luster, after dryness or unsuitable skin had made them look dull.

I am always running into this phenomenon. I can still remember my first meeting with a pearl wearer some years ago as if it were yesterday. A young woman appeared in our gallery, gave me the name of the person who had sent her, and asked very politely if I could re-string her pearls, and how long it would take. I said between two and three weeks. She seemed stunned, as though my answer was unthinkable. Her reaction surprised me, and I was about to take my leave when she opened her hand to reveal her pearls, saying: "These pearls belonged to my grand mother, I have worn them every day since they came into my possession, they are a part of myself!" Then, as if to give me a second chance, she placed the pearls to her neck, and looked at me questioningly.

GABRIELE WEINMANN, *"I have not forgotten the necklace of pearls, I feel them dancing on my skin..." Three necklaces in gold, Tahiti pearls, Akoya cultured pearls, white and*

blue brilliants, Biwa pearls, star sapphire, white and blue brilliants, "South Sea" pearls, white and blue brilliants

In front of me was a magnificent cascade of white pearls.

In front of me was this interplay between pearls and skin.

In front of me was this phenomenon whose explanation remains a mystery.

I was enchanted, and gave her the name of "pearl wearer". One thing was clear: my Sunday was to be dedicated to the pearls, the necklace simply had to be re-strung...

Those of you who have succumbed to the magic of pearls even only once will have experienced such things, and will experience them again. Of course, the moisture content of the specific skin type, as well as the acidity of some skins also have a role to play, both positive and negative. However, this does not explain the mystical exchange that can take place between pearls and skin.

The fact that, to this day, pearls have been unchallenged can be explained solely by these phenomena.

It is right to talk about the pure beauty of a classic pearl necklace worn by the ideal woman; equally you can talk about the pure beauty of a woman wearing the pearl necklace that is right for her. The affirmation applies in both senses: good reason to maintain the traditions surrounding pearls.

WIGBERT STAPFF, *"magical fascination". Necklace and ring in gold with Biwa pearl, brilliants and precious stones*

Many jewelry designers, goldsmiths and gem cutters have not dared to experiment with pearls out of respect for such an admirable work of nature. Is it really disrespectful to try anyway?

Mikimoto succeeded in culturing pearls some hundred years ago because he was prepared to experiment. And so, at the turn of the twenty-first century, it is our duty to use these marvelous results as the basis for our own continuing experiments. To do this, we must be brave in trying to improve the imperfect results of pearl culture with the help of new ideas and skills, in order to reduce the existing gap between pearls and people employed in the industry who treat them with reverence.

WIGBERT STAPFF and GABRIELE WEINMANN,
"A game whose rules have never been established in writing..." Necklace of multicolored "South Sea" pearls, interchangeable clasp in gold with brilliants and opal inlays, ring "between two fingers" in gold with brilliants and "emerald cut", "tapered" baguette and "princess cut" diamonds

Cultured pearls often present a cleft, meaning that the nucleus has not been entirely enclosed in the mother-of-pearl lining. The nucleus implant has not been totally covered by the oyster. This is especially true in the culture of the large Pacific and Australian pearls.

Last year in Bali I came across an incredibly beautiful necklace made from surprisingly large Australian pearls, almost all presenting a

WIGBERT STAPFF, *"Wounds caused by a miracle of nature filled with multicolored opals." Necklace of Southern pearls, gold, opal inlays, boulder opals*
▼

WIGBERT STAPFF, *"If pearls are a gift from the gods, polishing them must surely be auspicious." Pendant-brooch in gold, an exceptionally large "South Sea" pearl with opal and dumortierite inlays, brilliant, onyx quartz, opal and dumortierite set in the gold, obsidian*
▶

cleft; for the first time I felt the compulsion to stop these 'wounds' . In my mind, I imagined filling in the 'wounds' of this natural miracle with sparkling multicolored opals.

I listened to my interlocutor, a natural pearl wearer, as she talked to me about "her" pearls, trying to defend their so-called imperfection. Realizing just how captivated I was by the sight in front of me, she said: "Perhaps you will find

▲ WIGBERT STAPFF, *"Return the sea to the pearls". Necklace in Akoya cultured pearls, gold, opal inlays, polished boulder opal in imaginative shapes*

▶ WIGBERT STAPFF, *"The union of two very different elements of nature." Pendant in gold, Tahiti pearl, pink quartz, brilliant, opal inlay, necklace of Akoya cultured pearls*

a way of perfecting the imperfect works of nature". I tried to justify these images in my mind, asking myself the how and why... I reflected on it. On the return journey, I worked out how to realize my dreams. If pearls are a gift from the gods, polishing them must surely be auspicious.

Pearls have always been pierced, not only to be secured and strung, but also to be inlaid with gemstones set in metal. They are also polished in order to fit different mounts.

I discussed my idea with my partner Wigbert Stapff, who polishes the imaginative shapes of the gemstones for our jewelry, and is an expert in the field of opal inlays. He was interested in my idea, and so we bought the necklace and he began to experiment. The first attempts soon took on visible form. He polished the 'wounds' and filled the clefts with opal inlays.

The decision to use opals for the first attempts had been easy. We are no less fascinated by opals than we are by pearls, since, like the latter, their luster and radiance depend on light and hue. What sense is there then in opposing the union of two elements, by nature different, if their respective radiance attracts equally? And what happens if you combine pearls and transparent and multicolored gemstones? What does a pearl feel once her 'wounds' have been stopped with a polished diamond? Will the attraction of a perfect pearl be undermined if the gemstone gives it another form? Magical incarnations.

We work with the aim of making magical dreams become reality. Our experiments are not based on the desire to perfect a beauty that is already perfect by nature, nor on that of making the classic pearl unfashionable. Perfect beauty is neither unrivaled, nor everlasting. Our desire is to be daring and launch out into the unknown, looking for a result with its own unique fascination.

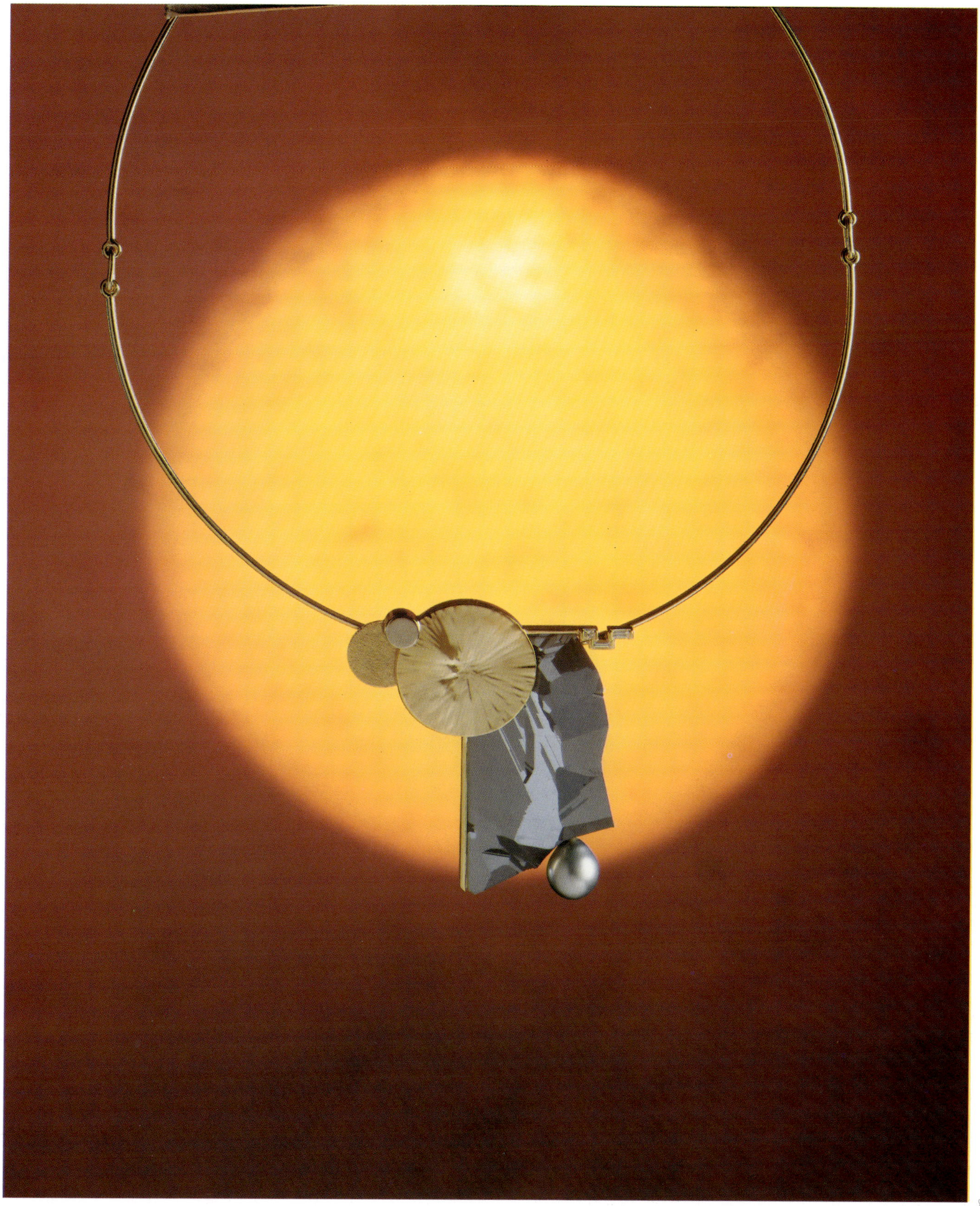

◂ *"Pearls... Gathered carefully In the fingertips. Combined with jewels Resplendent with gold, Wear them around your neck, On your breast! Allah's raindrops, Ripened in their modest casket."*
Goethe The East-West Divan *Book by Suleika*

▴ JAN VANSCHOENWINKEL, *yellow and white gold, brilliants, Tahiti pearl and a piece of solar cell. In this new "Sunshine" collection the sun, worshipped by different cultures for thousands of years, reigns supreme. The presence of the gold disk establishes a link between the past, the present and the future*

BERND MUNSTEINER, *brooch-pendant in gold and angel hair (rutile quartz)*

CHAPTER II

The Gemstones of the Future

In collaboration with BERND MUNSTEINER

First of all, let us think about minerals, the natural treasures of the earth. Under difficult conditions, and often only after hard labor, are they brought up out of the ground and into the daylight. We can only hope that, in the future, enough minerals will be found in the different mines around the globe.

The process of cutting gemstones begins with the minerals in their natural form. Saint Thomas Aquinas said: "to put the sparkle into reality."

Today, however, I would like to talk about the form of gemstones, the different cutting techniques and jewelry design.

But what do we expect?

The poet Goethe wrote: " Form is a sign of live development..."

The rules of design say that: "the visible form of things is the external expression of an interior meaning..." (Duden).

"Today we understand design to mean the individualistic search for form, the understandable and perceptible expression of man for whom the pursuit of an idea accidentally leads to a work..." (School of Design).

Design is not only a technical process, but a mental one.

Agate is a form of quartz that appears in various colors – from brown to red to grayish-blue and black – depending on where it is found. It also has a distinct grain and large white bands. The bands are layered concentrically around a cavity in the rock, much like the rings on a tree trunk. It is always difficult opening one of these druses, since you never know what you are going to find inside. First, I have to identify the various structures and bands of color. Then I choose a section to work on, which already sets certain limits as to what can be done with the stone. I learn to take advantage of what nature has created by chance, and to eliminate any kind of arbitrariness. This dialogue between the mineral and myself is essential before I can start to work. Since 1963 I have been searching for new agates with new shapes and forms. My interest in the subject goes back to the time when my professor, Karl Schollmayer, asked me how I would interpret a modern cameo. At first I tried cutting graphical, two-dimensional motifs in agate – primarily onyx and carnelian – but I also tried to bring out the naturally-occurring differences in the layers and bands by creating three-dimensional forms. Although my methods have changed constantly over the years, these two elements are still as important in my work today as they were at the beginning.

For many years now, I have been making annual trips to Brazil in search of the minerals that I need. Different minerals, such as aquamarine, tourmaline, amethyst, citrine, garnet and rock-crystal, have different properties, and the artist who works with them must be sensitive to their respective characteristics. I am particularly fascinated by their color, their respective ability to refract light and their brilliance. Light is an essential element in our lives and I take my inspiration from the way it plays on form.

Trying to find out what effects various kinds of reflection have is a fascinating business. Free sculptures derive from the interplay and juxtaposition of different shapes, surfaces, curves, incisions and facets. The realization of an idea using crystals is always determined by the structure of the stone. When two crystals have different structures, the results will never be the same.

My first works in cut crystals are called "Reflective Perspectives". These were followed by "Natural Movement", where I consciously tried to make crystalline structures and inclusions an integral part of my design. When I am working with crystals of more than one color, I find three-dimensional cutting – for example the optical separation of colors – a useful element of design.

The problems and considerations that arise when you are cutting precious stones cannot be seen in isolation. They have to be viewed together with the chosen metal and the piece of jewelry. At the same time, when an artist thinks about a piece of jewelry, or precious stones or even metals, he cannot afford to neglect the human element, the person who will eventually wear his work.

To my mind, jewelry is an expression of individual personality. There is no other art form with which we literally come into such close contact.

The alchemists of old equated gold with the human intellect and the sun. I consider it to be one of the most fascinating of all metals, and usually choose yellow gold for my work. In the case of jewelry, the main emphasis is on the cut stone while the precious metal acts as a support. The precious stone or sculpture is set in gold, platinum or silver; these are an extension of the original design and form a consummate whole. The colors and the effect of the light on the piece of jewelry are like signals. Each new design is the result of an ongoing process. For me, analysis of this process continually results in new experiences, which in turn inspire me to keep searching and developing my designs.

The metamorphosis of crystals: the transformation of a hexagonal crystal into a new and unrestrained form designed by myself. The creation of a new, perceptible space, appropriate to the choice of material, the discovery of illusionary processes through the reflection of light. The three-dimensionality of sculpture opens up greater possibilities for design. Unlike a piece of jewelry, it has no direct relation to the eventual wearer. Free-form sculpture aims to create a relationship with itself, the surrounding space and the viewer.

JÖRG MUNSTEINER, *ring in gold, red tourmaline (rubellite) and morganite*

BERND MUNSTEINER, *"Reflective Perspectives", exceptional peridot weighing 53.92 carats. Unquestionably a "gemstone of the future"*

The only constraint is that larger crystals of the required purity, such as rock-crystal, rutile quartz, citrine, amethyst and aquamarine, rarely occur naturally.

I will begin by talking about the minerals which form part of the earth's treasure, brought to the surface by hard labor, to sparkle in the daylight, in the sincere hope that our planet will continue to produce this raw material, so that gem cutters like myself will be able to go on creating in the future.

The minerals that I work with are more than 200

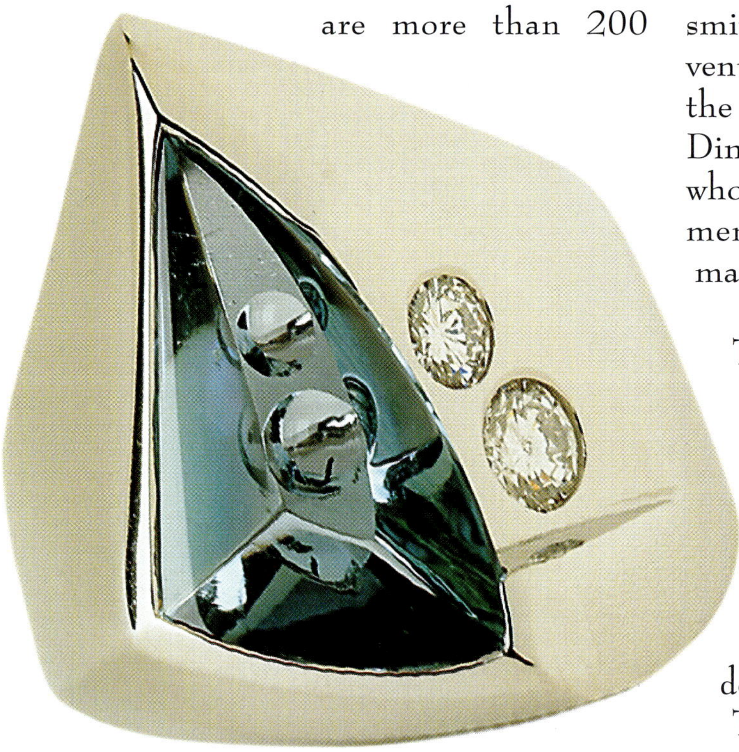

JÖRG MUNSTEINER, *ring with aquamarine and diamonds*

million years old and were present when the planet was born. They belong to different crystal systems and therefore have a variety of wonderful shapes.

This is my starting point. The inspiration begins with the crystal which I hold in my hand, as I study the mineral, its color and purity, the inclusions, and its opaqueness or transparency. Then I begin my work, using the different proportions, rhythms and contrasts that lead to a good design.

The last word goes to Oscar Wilde: "We live in a period in which only superfluous things are necessary to us."

During the structural and cultural changes of the last 500 years, unlike art, music or architecture, gem cutting as a craft made no decisive progress.

There have been many changes in the creation of jewels, and many a famous goldsmith. Here are just a few: the Italian Benvenuto Cellini (1500-1571), influential in the late Renaissance period, the Schwabian Dinglinger at the end of the 17th century, who worked for the Sachsen Court, and, as mentioned earlier, Fabergé (who worked mainly for the Zsar of Russia).

The famous goldsmiths René Lalique, Wilhelm of Cranach, Tiffany, Georg Jensen and others were among the exponents of Art Nouveau *(Jugendstil)* in the early 1900s. In the 20th century, many important artists like Picasso, Braque, Dali, Wunderlich and more have turned their attention to jewelry design.

Today the world is full of remarkable artists making pieces of jewelry, many of which can be seen in museums around the globe. But what do we expect from the design of a gemstone or piece of jewelry? The poet Goethe wrote: "The form of an object is the fruit of internal experience."

The rules of design say: "The visible form of things is the external expression of an interior meaning."

"Today we understand design to mean the individualistic search for form, the understandable and perceptible working out of an idea." (School of Design).

Tom Munsteiner, *ring in platinum, 6.70 carats of aquamarine and diamond*

tion of precious stones is part of this process, and will continue to be part of it in the future.

In my opinion, it is the high technical quality of our products and their innovative design that will enable them to survive. This innovation will play a decisive role in the creation of new articles and designer collections in conformity with the fashion industry and its trends.

Individual creations will take the lead, as they always have done in the past. In this light, gem and jewelry-work will remain part of our cultural heritage. At the top will be the unique piece, the work of art.

I served my apprenticeship with my father, a gem cutter who had himself learned

Design is not only a technical process, but also a mental one.

Since the 1960s our lifestyle and our whole social and global perspective has changed considerably, and so has our mindset.

"Egocentricity" and "individuality" are the slogans of today. The search for rapid change, for renewal, for the expansion of scientific frontiers are the themes that will occupy us in the future. A new revolution has started in the industrial and technical fields all over the world. Labor is expensive in the western world. Gem cutting and the commercializa-

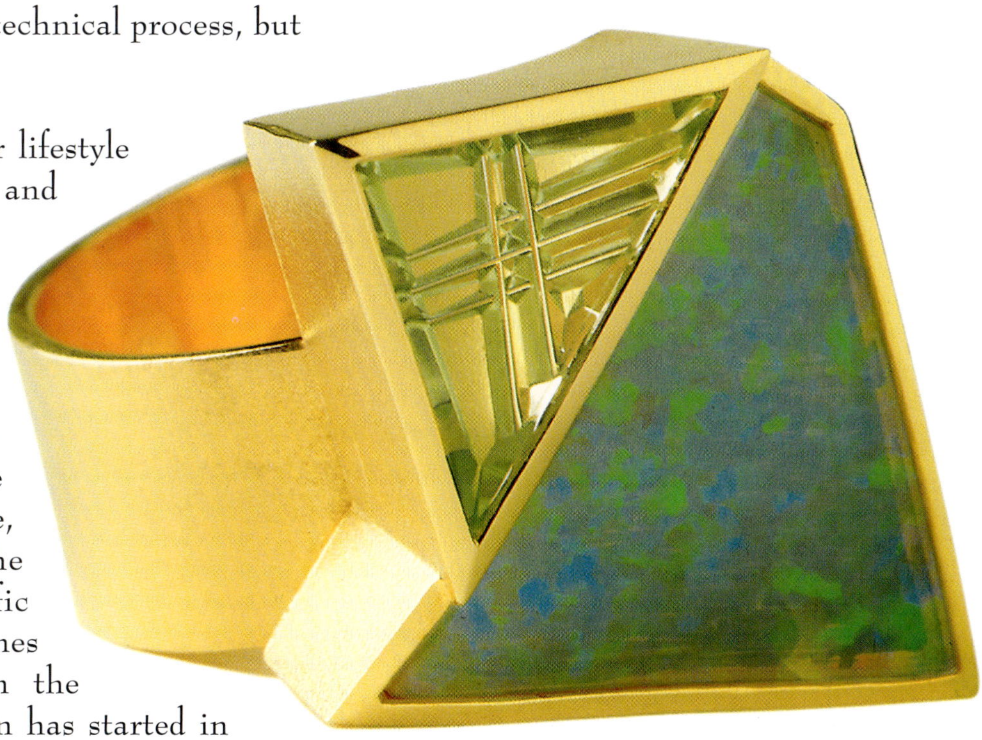

Bernd Munsteiner, *ring in gold, yellow/green beryl and boulder opal*

his trade from his father. In 1963 I studied at the University of Pforzheim in the Black Forest. There, I began to experiment with new designs in gemstones. This was a completely new subject at the time. My teachers were Prof. Karl Schollmayer, Prof. Klaus Ullrich and Erich Frey.

I understand any personal adornment, any work of jewelry, to be an artistic testimony of our present time, an individual statement as a means of communication. Jewelry therefore stands out as an expression of personality.

Since time immemorial, the sensation of eroticism has been at the base of any personal adornment and this remains so even today. In this way, it remains as a part of our culture.

The minerals I work with have been under the ground for more than 200 million years, and as they come out of the earth, they present wonderful crystals, each (naturally) faceted according to its crystal system. It is from here that I start my creative work, which may perhaps remain as that for another 100 or even several hundred years.

My inspiration therefore derives from the rough piece in my hands and an idea is born. I am guided by a certain natural feeling, a sensibility for the specific stone material. What counts is also the color of the mineral, the clearness or the inclusions, and some other things. They will all be considered at the time of composition: the proportions, the rhythm, and contrasting shapes to lead to a good design.

The theme, as a message, could have many faces: they will show reflections, perspectives, movements of lines, cutting in to the crystals, curving light effects, etc. The final work ends as a summarizing of many ideas, thoughts, effects and visions, finally collected and presented in a piece of gem material, which may transmit a message to someone. Only in this way may we achieve an artistic work that will also be a permanent part of our culture.

The gem cutter is faced with the raw material, from which he creates, and, to use

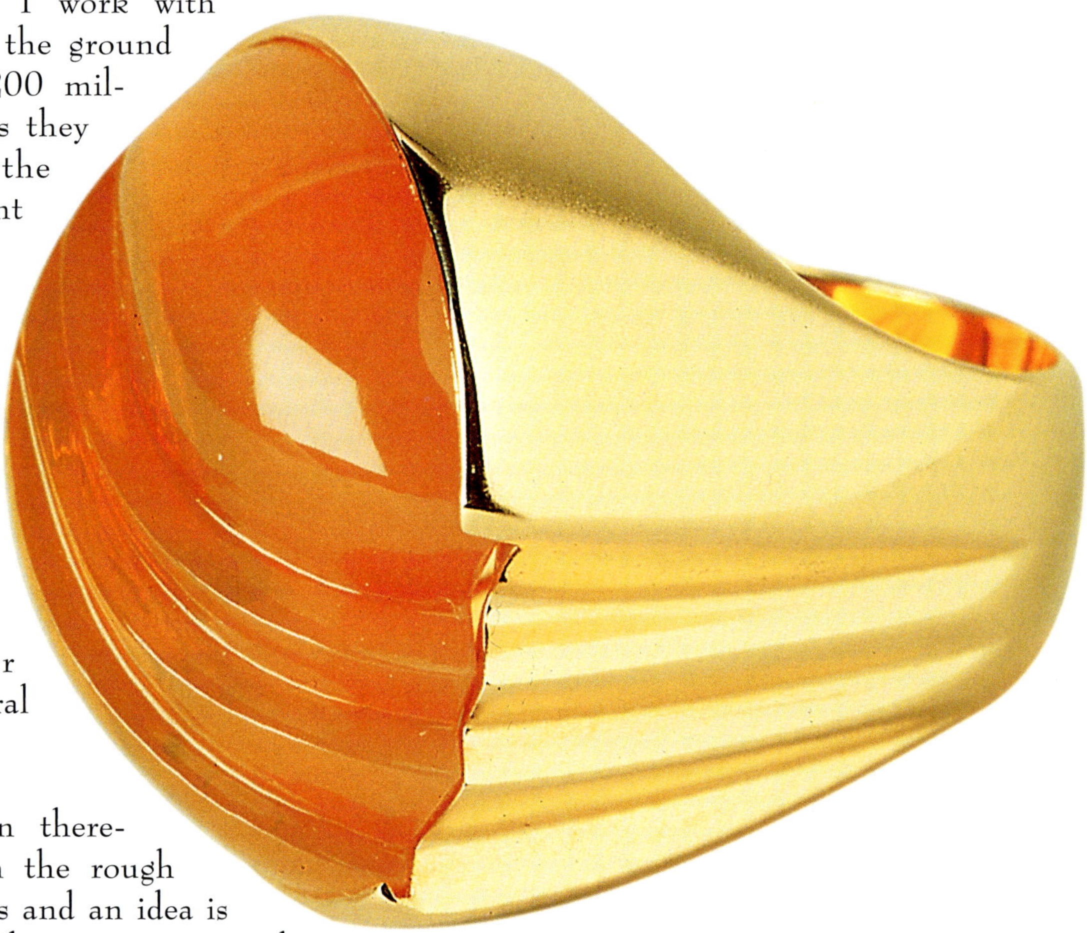

JÖRG MUNSTEINER, *ring in gold and fire opal weighing 50.00 carats*

JUTTA MUNSTEINER, *brooch in gold and platinum with an aquamarine of 44.93 carats and lapis lazuli. Made by Tom Munsteiner*

Saint Thomas Aquinas' expression, "puts the sparkle back into reality".

Before I tackle the subject of gem cutting, I would like to take a retrospective look at its history.

It is hard to believe, but 30,000 years ago men were already working stone, using the best material available at the time, to make tools and weapons; this was the so-called Stone Age.

The principal methods were:
Engraving and carving the precious stone;
Cutting the precious stone.

The Sumerians, the Babylonians and the Assyrians used these two methods to make cylindrical seals some 5000-6000 years before our time.

More recently, the Greeks and the Romans took up the art of sculpting gemstones, producing some beautiful works, such as the famous "Gemma Augusta" or the "Tassa Farnese", now in the art museum in Vienna.

Until the 19th century, cameos and intaglios predominantly featured classical motifs.
It was the famous goldsmith Carl Fabergé (1873-1920), working mainly for the Russian Court, who brought new ideas and motifs into the art of gem cutting. His motifs of leaves, flowers, butterflies and animals were inspired by nature. These motifs are still in evidence in contemporary production.

The oldest cut gemstone dates back thousands of years, and is called "cabochon" because it looks like a button (hence the Latin word "gem"). Its radius is equal to its height. Numerous attempts have been made to grind, smooth and polish the surface.

The faceting and polishing of transparent crystals began in earnest in the Middle Ages, the regular geometrical shape conforming to the general style of that particular era. With the invention of the horizontal grinding wheel in 1476 came the practice of giving the gems symmetrical facets.

The so-called "diamond cut" emerged during the 17th and 18th centuries, in the baroque and rococo periods, and has subsequently been perfected. Most recently, the "ideal cut" has been obtained by acting on the optical proportions of the facets.

Industrialization and the possibility of achieving perfection have given rise to the commercialization of precious stones, and gems are being cut and polished with increasing speed. However, creation is still the fruit of individual effort.

JÖRG MUNSTEINER, *pendant necklace in gold, diamonds, rough polychrome tourmaline and cut red tourmaline (rubellite)*

CHRISTINE HAFERMALZ-WHEELER, *"Ruapehu", brooch-pendant in gold and silver with black pearl from the Cook Islands, Mexican opal and agate signed by Bernd Munsteiner. This jewel represents the eruption of the largest volcano in New Zealand*

CHRISTINE HAFERMALZ-WHEELER, *"City of Snails", necklace in yellow and white gold, Paraiba tourmalines, white and colored diamonds and an aquamarine cut by Bernd Munsteiner. This pendant represents Waitemata, the port at Auckland*

▸ MICHAEL ZOBEL, *pendant in gold and platinum with 65.99 carats of aquamarine cut by Bernd Munsteiner*

MICHAEL ZOBEL, *brooch-pendant in gold and silver with angel hair (rutile quartz), 5.11 carats of rough diamond and 10 brilliants of 0.10 carat*

MICHAEL ZOBEL, *ring in gold and silver with angel hair (rutile quartz), rough diamond and five brilliants*

ERWIN PAULY, *"Aida". A Brazilian agate represents Aida's head, surrounded by meaningful symbols such as the platinum headgear decorated with 15 yellow sapphires and three leaves in peridot extracted from a deposit near Aswan, set in 18 carats of yellow gold. The loose cut is surrounded by a sphere of yellow gold weighing 18 carats. The upper part is taken up with two pyramids. The first, in platinum with a yellow sapphire, is dedicated to the god Ra, and the second, in diamond set in platinum, is dedicated to infinity and eternity. The pyramid whose apex points downwards, a blue sapphire, is surrounded by platinum and yellow gold, symbolizing the destinies of Aida and Radam. This cameo is a symbolic, verbal and sonorous echo of the unforgettable final chord of the opera*

ERWIN PAULY, *"Parsifal". The main protagonists of Wagner's opera are represented in this cameo. The blue and white streaked Brazilian agate measuring 60 mm by 50 mm in the lower part shows Parsifal with his bow and the sacred arrow. Behind the swan's wings are the King and Kundry, Gral's female messenger. On the right the young flower children look on. The scene is dominated by the lake and the door to Gral's castle which are suspended near the sacred arrow. On the lower part of the watch in 18 carat gold, Gral's lake in platinum is decorated with brilliants and blue sapphires. Crowning the watch are the three towers of the castle in platinum and diamonds. "Parsifal" is an important glyptic piece for cameo and classical music lovers*

ERWIN PAULY, *"astral horse", rock-crystal, gold and black tourmaline*

ERWIN PAULY, *"Etalon", large-scale cameo (200 × 150 mm), on display in Houston, Texas*

MIEKE GOVAERTS, *necklace in gold and aquamarine*

CHAPTER III

The Neo-Classicists

In collaboration with

MIEKE GOVAERTS & TIZIANO ANDORNO

The sublimation of the encounter: the magical moment in which two disparate elements confront each other before uniting to give life to ideas and experience.

Our search centers on the emotion that can be expressed through the allegorical use of color, the exaltation of natural forms, the expansion or compression of solid masses; and it is based on unique ideas and materials evoking the interaction, the sound, the movement, the transformation, and everything else that combines to create a totality of elements that are both distinct and complementary...

Just like us!

Talking about oneself or simply describing oneself is always difficult, which is why we have asked Mario Lupi to do it for us.

My activities have brought me into contact with all kinds of people: some who manage to find inspiration in interesting shapes, others who try to copy, modifying the existing object as they see fit, and many more who openly copy through a total lack of imagination and personal stimulation; few, on the other hand, all too few, who are genuinely able to create.

Tiziano Andorno and Mieke Govaerts are among the small number of creators in the field of jewelry-making to produce forms that are always new, original, unusual. They use gemstones, the source of dreams, from tourmalines to black diamonds, aquamarines to sapphires, rubies to quartz in its natural, crystalline form, or cut to show off its intrinsic qualities.

Tiziano produces abstract forms that belong to the domain of *Extrême* jewelry. These forms are linked to a long series of inspirations rooted in strong feelings that the intellect subsequently apprehends.

Jewels are the reflection of the changes that take place in our daily life, the result of an intense search that projects the piece of jewelry, as it is experienced by the collective imagination, into another dimension. The intelligent combination of dynamism, strength, originality, provocation, irony and chaos generates jewels that are unique and impossible to reproduce, suitable for people that can identify with the emotions experienced by their creator.

In his infinite geometries, Mieke represents the other aspect of the *Extrême*. These

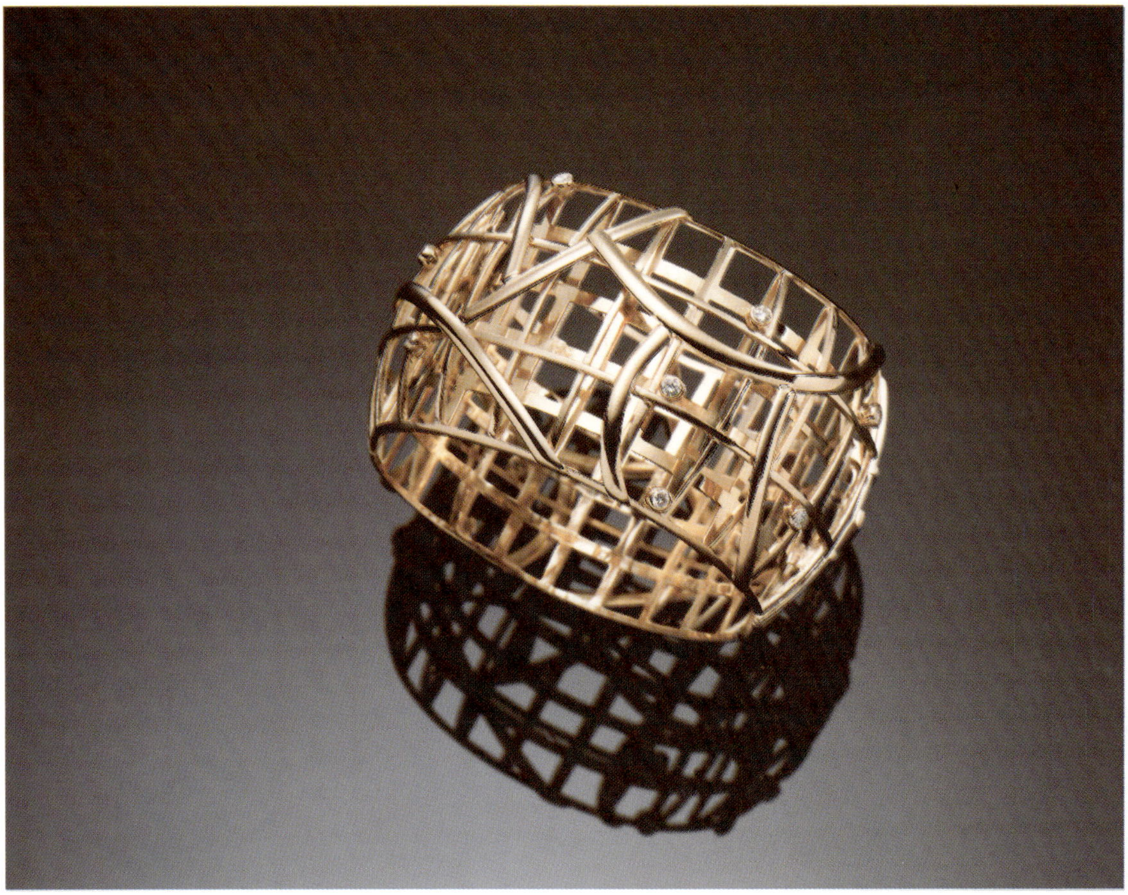

MIEKE GOVAERTS, *bracelet in gold and diamonds*

TIZIANO ANDORNO, *bracelet in multicolored gold*

TIZIANO ANDORNO, *gold ring with multicolored stones*

TIZIANO ANDORNO, *gold bracelet with multicolored stones of all shapes*

patterns of intersecting and overlying elements give rise to marvelous forms, ordered and inspired by a creative mind in perfect harmony with the rationalization of idea and form that allows for the use of every known stone.

Together they theorize the neo-classical; they contribute to the development of the jewelry myth by paving the way for their many followers in the third millennium.

Those who know them as well as I do would no doubt describe them as order and disorder, the angel and the devil, the sacred and the profane, and nitrogen and glycerin.

TIZIANO ANDORNO, *ring in yellow and white gold with multicolored precious stones*

TIZIANO ANDORNO, *necklace in multicolored gold, diamonds and rough aquamarine*

▸

MARCELLO PIZZARI, *"Libellule", unique piece in gold, diamonds and precious and fine stones*

 RCM *of* LORENZO RICCI, *exceptional brooch in gold and blue and yellow diamonds*

RCM *of* LORENZO RICCI, *gold bracelet with multicolored diamonds, white, yellow, purple and lilac*

MOUAWAD, *set made from black Tahiti pearls, gold and diamonds*

MOUAWAD, *set of jewels in white gold with 94.50 carats of circular, oval and baguette cut diamonds and 87.62 carats of Burmese rubies.*
Mouawad, a passionate lover of beauty and rarity. Robert Mouawad is a demanding aesthete. He respects extreme standards of quality and beauty out of love for his work. He is driven by a desire that is strong, almost totally absorbing. The design for every set, necklace, bracelet or brooch is subject to his knowing gaze. He is after pure beauty alone; his style is personal, timeless, designed to suit any and every woman.
His creations are like a magic rite in continual repetition; like love, like pleasure, like an unending desire for riches and refinement.

For a woman, jewelry is the ultimate beauty product: it is the mirror of her desires, her character and her mood.
Rubies represent love, fire, passion, the strength of an amorous woman who will do anything for the man she loves. Diamonds symbolize purity, the sparkling light that illuminates all mysteries without destroying them. Emeralds are for determined women who know what they want and get it with the gentleness and charm which make them so powerful.
Sapphires and aquamarines evoke space, escapism, the dreams of women who believe that they can have it all. Pearls are the symbol of class and sobriety and live with women, needing the heat and rhythm of their body to survive.

◂ MOUAWAD, *set in yellow gold, brilliant cut, baguette cut and marquise cut diamonds weighing 103.48 carats with 144.37 carats of cabochon rubies*

▴ MOUAWAD, *set in yellow gold and diamonds*

MELITA CAPUANO, *the historic wedding ring created for the Capuano family for several generations*

"A ring of ivy..."
It is a singular jewel, a piece of goldsmithery conceived and realized with the greatest care and attention by the artisan goldsmith Giovanni Tarriziani in the 1930s. Ivy is the symbol of faithfulness in love, and it is for this reason that the author dedicated his creation to his wife Jeanne, his inspiring muse.
The unusual shape of the ring has been conceived to fit the anatomy of the finger. The large leaves adhere to one another as if to "crown" the powerful symbolism of attachment, of a solemn promise, because ivy defies being uprooted once it has taken hold.
The detailed chisel work and the numerous brilliants on each leaf reflect the love and care with which the work was carried out.
Moreover, ivy carries multiple meanings deriving from history. Poets and conquerors were once crowned with it as a sign of glory; and, like evergreen, it is the symbol of enduring and eternal love.
The woman who wears this ring must certainly be strong and secure in the choice she makes.

MELITA CAPUANO, *the famous "Capuano" wedding ring created by Giovanni Tarriziani in 1950. Look at the history of this object*

Andrea Frahm

 Melita Capuano, *"Butterfly", brooch-pendant in white and yellow gold with diamonds and sapphires*

MELITA CAPUANO, *brooch in white gold and diamonds*

MELITA CAPUANO, *"Rose", brooch in white and yellow gold, coral, emeralds and diamonds*

ANDREA GALASSINI, *bracelet from the series "geometry", in white gold and keystone cut diamonds*

KEVORK APOSHIAN, *pendant, earrings and rings in yellow and white gold with diamonds, rubies and blue and yellow sapphires*

◂ VIVIANE DEBBAS, *brooch in gold, pearls and diamonds.*
In 1991, Viviane Debbas fixed upon Paris to launch her first collections and her boutique. She developed a distinctive style, born of a combination of East and West, generosity and enchantment, elegance and singularity, tradition and modernity.
This ensemble still represents the qualities of the label that bears her name.
Two years later, she transferred her boutique to the center of Beirut, and since then she has organized regular exhibitions in numerous European cities (Paris, London, Cannes, Marbella) and in the Middle East. Due to her exacting taste and standards Viviane Debbas constantly renews her creations, on each occasion presenting unusual models. From sumptuous jewels to pieces suitable for various occasions, Viviane Debbas' creations are a pleasure to look at and the expression of the love felt by a creator for her work ▾

VIVIANE DEBBAS, *"Flowers"*, *brooch in gold and blue, yellow and purple diamonds*

MELKON HAGOPIAN, *"Birds"*, *brooch in yellow gold. This is a unique piece composed of a baroque "South Sea" pearl, cabochon rubies and blue, green and yellow diamonds*

MARTA SENSIDONI

MELKON HAGOPIAN, *jewels in beaten yellow gold made exclusively by hand with baroque Japanese (Biwa) pearls and 4.16 carats of diamonds*

◄ANGELO SPINELLI, *"Hommage à Caravage" ("Tribute to Caravaggio"), pendant-brooch in yellow and white gold with enamel, pearls, diamonds, sapphires and two fire opals. This piece of jewelry can be transformed into a pendant using the upper and lower parts, whilst the center part can also be worn around the neck*

▲ANGELO SPINELLI, *earrings of white gold, diamonds and two emeralds of 140 carats, cut and engraved by the artist*

▲ De Grisogono, *the play of light-dark contrasts on this splendid ring, fascinating due to the harmony of the shapes and the delicacy of its setting in gray gold. It comprises 12 black diamonds weighing 50.00 carats set around a superb white emerald cut diamond of 7.00 carats. It is a unique piece*

▲
De Grisogono,
an exceptional collection of jewels made using black diamonds
◀ ▶

TIZIANA *and* MASSIMO ALOISIO, *"Saint Apollinaire", ring (and ciborium) in gold and diamonds, inspired by a detail of the ciborium at Saint Apollinaire in Ravenna*

CHAPTER IV

Architect-Jewelers

In collaboration with TIZIANA and MASSIMO ALOISIO

"The aim of architecture is to generate emotion.
Architectonic emotion occurs when the work resounds inside us in harmony
with a universe on whose laws we confer obedience, faith, respect."
(Le Corbusier)

This observation by the great 20th-century architect Le Corbusier encourages us to strive for a degree of aesthetic harmony in jewelry design that generates emotion.

Jewels have been, and still are more than simple ornaments, evaluated according to their preciousness or ability to enhance. They should evoke a feeling, a memory, expressing moral codes or lifestyle, and so become a symbol for the owner.

Faced with the "Kaos" of the universe, man has always studied its signs to apprehend its basic laws and structures, and to divide up the space to feel closer to nature.

Architecture: "construction according to a principle" (archi = principle/ tecton = builder).

Jewels were born as ornaments with a high symbolic value. It is reasonable to assume that the first jewels must have been leaves, stones, shells, or feathers dropped by a bird, and that man put on these elements in an attempt to feel part of a sometimes hostile environment.

With the arrival of metals, artistic expression in jewelry became more detailed and began to evoke symbols and mythological figures. Man used these figures to propitiate his co-inhabitant-nature; and, at the same time, to defend himself from it.

Architecture has undergone a similar developmental process, in its intense relationship to the environment in which it has evolved.

The influence which the various arts have had on one another is clearly visible throughout history. Architects of any one period have sometimes been influenced, if not directly inspired, by the skill of contemporary goldsmiths. Take, for example, the Byzantine period and its broad gold ceilings, or the gothic stained glass windows simulating, on a large scale, the reliquaries whose color and transparency derived from gemstones.

The study of nature, of what surrounds us and of what we have experienced, mediated by the capacity for synthesis and transposition, makes up the foundation of our work.

Practically speaking, the study and design of a piece of jewelry is similar in its composite structure to the process followed by the architect to solve the problems of design; and it involves spatial and structural analysis referable to architecture itself.

The sign conceals archetypes and symbols that confer on the structure both of the edi-

TIZIANA *and* MASSIMO ALOISIO, *"Dubrovnik", star-shaped pendant in gold, inspired by a stone decorative motif in a window of the Capuchin monastery in Dubrovnik*

fice and of the piece of jewelry a charm that surpasses its preciousness and beauty, insofar as the representation of absence arouses curiosity.

The Christian cross is just one example. The shape of the cross has been used by architects as the basic layout for the construction of churches, and goldsmiths have transformed it into a portable statement of faith.

The symbolic value of a work is determined by the expressive intention of its creator, and by his ability to maintain relations with the outside world; and it is only when the relationship between these two factors reaches osmosis that the work is able to preserve its expressive value over time.

The ceramic paintings from ancient Athens exemplify this concept. Here, the sign is the expression of an aesthetic serving a message that is both mythological and descriptive; and it has maintained its force and its ability to generate emotion over time.

Our desire for the future is to acknowledge the expressive and symbolic qualities of jewelry that have been at the base of this art from the outset; and we hope that in the new millennium the infinite means provided by modern technology are of assistance in the search for expression, leading creators to capture some of the "emotion" which the ancient civilizations managed to transmit through their work, and which can still be felt today.

Our thoughts can be summed up in the following sentence: *The sign is the origin of form. The material is the measure of the intensity of the desired message.*

TIZIANA *and* MASSIMO ALOISIO, *ring in gold, representing Ying and Yang*

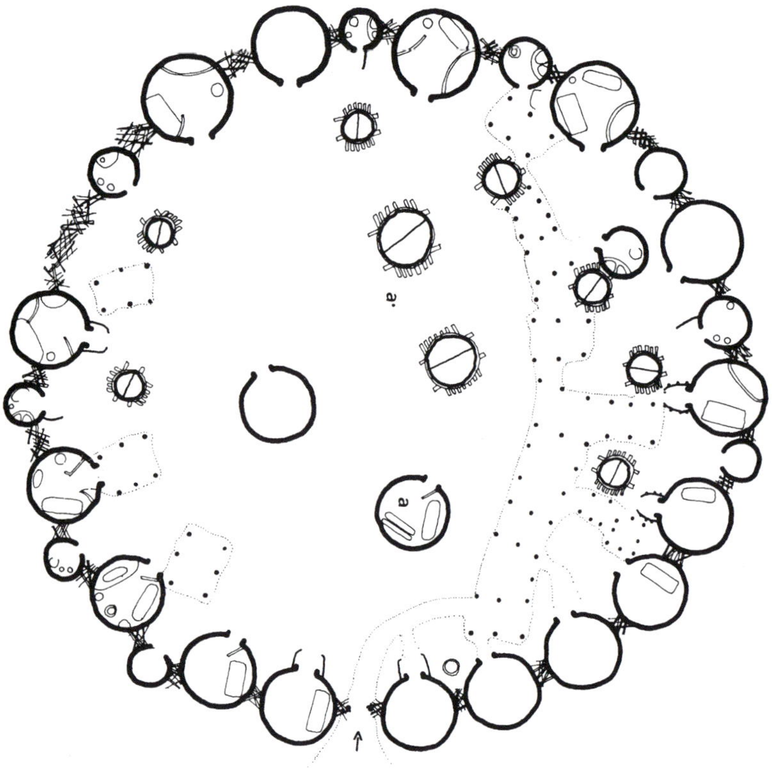

Tiziana *and* Massimo Aloisio,
"Kirkos", gold necklace (and design) inspired by the layout of a village, of a farm enclosure, Massa, Cameroon

TIZIANA *and* MASSIMO ALOISIO,
Attic medallions (photograph of the amphora which inspired the first medallion). "Fighters", gold brooch. Detail from an amphora, 4th century B.C., Claudio Faina Museum, Orvieto. "Bathers", gold brooch. Detail of young women taken from a red vase. C. 470 B.C., Metropolitan Museum, New York

ANTONIO SAPORITO, *"The Titans", for the silver service "The Lion", Florence*

Taking its name from the ancient Greek divinities, the tea and coffee service "The Titans" represents a new line in silverware. "The Titans" is a twisting cyclopean mass carved onto sides that are curved inside and out, full of corners and hidden recesses offering infinite perspectives which only the imagination is able to perceive. The tray with its original ergonomic form sets the tone for the line of the service.
The uniqueness of the set lies in the simplicity of its "harmonious center", the basic geometry of the main element, developed around the perimeter of each object, to which other information (separation and rotation) is added, forming an exceptionally light plastic and formal complex whole; the metal follows the form within the limitations of its resistance. The pieces consist of concave or convex planes inclined at different angles to harmonize the function, the plasticity and the light emanating from the silver itself... These are the characteristic elements of the service.
The handles made from dark walnut and different sized silver spheres are an additional original feature. This detail - decorative but also functional - makes the piece easy to pick up.
In another example of refined functionality, the sugar basin comprises two compartments designed to take different kinds of sugar.

ANTONIO SAPORITO,
"The Titans", for the silver service "The Lion", Florence
▼ ▶

Isabella Fa

CHAPTER V

Creators and Designers

In collaboration with

GREGOR TELGMANN

Jewels have a mystical dimension: they are an important feature of numerous fairy tales; and "fairy tale" is the term to describe Gregor Telgmann's stories – or rather dreams. Unlike the tales told by story-tellers, Gregor Telgmann's stories are all true. The goldsmith has owned a workshop in Kamen since 1969. Every piece of jewelry made by Telgmann is different. Every ring, every necklace, every bracelet is unique and carries his signature. He creates jewels on request, but he also gives form to his own personal experience. Ideas for new creations often come to him on holiday abroad. For example, he has created a brooch called "Reisterrassen" ("Rice Fields"), made from gold, a single sapphire and diamonds, inspired by the impressions of a journey which he describes as follows: "During our holiday in Indonesia, we passed rice fields, and we stopped in front of them to marvel at the irrigation systems. One day, I found myself looking down on one of these rice fields and admired the rice (cuttings and seedlings), the fields covered with water and the shoots; I could hear the sound of gentle murmuring caused by the breeze in the field. The sun was shining, and when I closed my eyes small stars appeared over some of the fields. I was so fascinated by this "spectacle" that it became forever imprinted on my memory. I was keen to create a piece of gold jewelry that reproduced this impression. First I drew a sketch, and that is how the brooch came into being. First I fashioned the metal to represent the rice fields that descend in a spiral towards the valley. The rice plants are recognizable on the surface. Conversely, I have smoothed over the parts that represent the submerged fields, the lagoons and the river. The sapphire, representing the fascinating play of the stars above the rice fields, I have placed towards the bottom. I have drained the water from the stagnant surface. Small brilliants suggest the sparkle of the flowing water. Then I displayed the brooch in my shop. A customer came in and told me that he recognized the place. He described the "spectacle" that I had seen in Indonesia. It was an unforgettable moment."

Extraordinary Creations

Gregor Telgmann's creativity is put to the test on a daily basis. He is asked to design and create personalized items. Gregor Telgmann studies the man or woman carefully, so that the jewel might reflect their personality. He roughs out a sketch in front of them straight away. To give a clearer idea, he adds the precious stones to the sketch and chooses their size. This is how the piece of jewelry is conceived. "For me, art is a question of skill. This means that I am unable to create unless I have done a preliminary sketch. The experiment does not necessarily fail without one, but it does not come from deep inside me," the goldsmith emphasizes. In the past, he used to draw three sketches in the presence of the client. "But I would be disappointed if he failed to choose my 'number one'. This is why I now do only one sketch. And I adopt the same approach to pieces of jewelry that have to be altered. Clients often ask me to remodel or alter the feel of a wedding ring or gemstones that have great sentimental value for them. It is important not only to listen carefully to these people, but also to penetrate their world and apprehend their desires. The goldsmith's task is to conceive and create a contemporary jewel that is personal, accentuates the personality of the person that wears it, and enhances the person all at once."

Sculptures

Gregor and Marianne Telgmann also display sculptures in the 34 showcases in their shop. "There is no law to say that a goldsmith must necessarily sculpt in metal. Even if bronze is used in jewelry-making, the difference lies in the use of other materials and the creation of larger objects." His tendency to create large forms dates from his five-year apprenticeship in the "Schönstätter Marienbrüder" studio in Vallendar, north-east of Koblenz. The studio is large and contains a number of master craftsmen with knowledge of a range of skills and techniques not exclusively to do with jewelry-making. Here, Gregor Telgmann also learnt how to mount gemstones, to chisel, cut, and work silver, as well as the techniques and procedures for sculpting metal – including how to make a model in different dimensions up to the scale of 1/1. Before sculpting, it is essential to master the raw material. "In general I use all materials: wood, silver, gold, platinum and even plastic. I have sufficient technical skill not to be restricted in the choice of raw material and its use. If I do not like it, or if I do not master the technique, I abandon it."

One of his recent sculptures is called "Nah und doch so fern" ("So near and yet so far"), a piece of goldsmithery made from gold and smoked quartz. It presents different images as it is rotated. "When I held the diamond-shaped smoked quartz on its rock-crystal base for the first time, I was fascinated by the perfection of the cut, as well as by the impression made by the reflections. By changing position, the viewer discovers different parts of the body that were formerly hidden." His most famous sculpture in Kamen is the "Die Quelle" fountain ("The Spring"), now a familiar element in the town's market square. Gregor Telgmann has no technical preference. "I would not want to create only large objects, but nor would I want to create only jewels. There are so many ideas and emotions that I would like to express. This is why I am pleased to master the use of new materials."

Gregor Telgmann has received numerous prizes for his creations. However, in spite of his success, the goldsmith has kept to the facts and preserved his modesty. The Telgmanns have always considered the pleasure of jewels, design and art to be of utmost importance. "For years we have tried to make our art and our culture accessible to the population", explains Marianne Telgmann. To this end, they have organized numerous exhibitions: "Ballett und Brillanten" ("Ballet and Brilliants") in collaboration with the school of dance; "Renate Hetkamp" of Bergkamen, the exhibition "Couronnes" from the "Abeler" collection in Wuppertal; "Schmuck der Südsee" ("Gems of the Pacific") at the "Linden" museum in Stuttgart; the exhibition "Fabergé et Icônes" on the occasion of the visit of the Russian cultural attaché Alexander Masslokow and the members of the Moscow Bolschoi Theatre; or else the evening event "Pierres précieuses" to coincide with the presentation of a bridal dress made from platinum to mark the 25th anniversary of their shop. During the running of the exhibition "De Beers Gems and Design – Diamonds of Today" in 1997, they organized "Diamonds Live". The guests spent a splendid evening admiring not only the unique pieces created by the Telgmanns, but also the "De Beers" competition-winners, including a creation by Alexandra Telgmann, Gregor's older daughter. For the competition "Facetten der Persönlichkeit" ("Facets of personality") she had made "Spirit Sun", a piece of gold jewelry incorporating cut diamonds. It is a versatile jewel: it can be worn as a necklace, as a brooch or as a buckle. Alexandra Telgmann has received public acclaim not only for her creations, but also for the extraordinarily successful presentation organized in collaboration with her two sisters Dorothée and Stephanie. The latter, the youngest in the family, is successfully following in her father's footsteps. Her design for the ring "Utopia" won her first prize in the "Idar-Oberstein International Competition for Jewelry and Gemstone Design – Youth Section". "The organization of all these evening events is only possible with the help of the whole family. Our daughters love jewelry. They have presented our creations with natural charm..." says Gregor Telgmann and his wife adds: "We enjoy doing new things, because art is not only about hosting parties, but also about finding people who are enthusiastic about what we do. The invitations that we send to our clients to keep in touch allow them to share our enthusiasm."

Portrait of Gregor Telgmann

Gregor Telgmann, born in Werne in 1940, learned the trade of watchmaking like his father and grandfather before him. His preference for design and creation led him to join the corporation of goldsmiths, where he was received as a master craftsman in 1968. In 1976 he was recognized as an artist by the Art and Design section of the "Specialist Professional School" of Cologne. Since 1978, he has been a member of the association "Who's Who in the Arts". His artistic talent and his work have been admired and rewarded at exhibitions and in international publications. Gregor Telgmann is a member of the association of Christian goldsmiths and artists.

Future Projects

I have all sorts of ideas, unusual and fantastic ideas which find expression in sketches. I am inspired by nature: I like all beautiful things and music. I draw inspiration from these things to create new works of art. The ability to observe, feel and absorb impressions: these are the indispensable qualities for harmonizing the material and the imagined form of the work of art. My personality must be legible in my work in order that the piece takes life and begins to express something to the observer. There are a lot of ideas that I would like to realize. My hands – guided by my thoughts, my feelings, my imagination and my skill as a craftsman – create pieces of jewelry out of precious materials.

For example, I dream about making a silver case decorated with precious stones.

STEPHANIE TELGMANN, *"Utopia", ring*

This ring won first prize at the International Competition for Jewelry and Gemstone Design - Youth Section - in Idar Oberstein. Ring in gold and silver. The concavities in the ball are set with sapphires and emeralds which can oscillate with a simple movement of the hand. This ring, with its novel and creative conception, is a hymn to optimism. Designed and made by Stephanie Telgmann (aged 20).

At the moment, I am trying to create a bronze sculpture with a fountain.

With regard to jewelry, it is opal which inspires me the most. Moreover, I prefer "Spirit Sun" and "Context Cut" cuts.

My next work will be a Via Crucis. Religious art is very important to me. On several occasions now I have helped to decorate churches in Germany and abroad: altarpieces, crosses or liturgical vessels.

For me, being a goldsmith is a job for life. We are all familiar with jewelers' boutiques with their windows, symbols of beauty and luxury. The real secret is hidden behind this façade, far from the world of commerce, in the heart of the goldsmith's atelier. The profession is a kind of vocation, a passion, mission or message, but at the same time it is an art. Its aim is to reconcile dream and reality and to give concrete form to this dualism through the aesthetic. My message always centers on the human being.

I consider the jewel to be a sort of ambassador for a world which makes use of symbols to communicate deep feelings. The jewel is not a superficial expression of our age.

It is with impatience and joy that I await what the future will bring and I rejoice in new challenges. Art affects men the world over and facilitates understanding between people.

ALEXANDRA TELGMANN, *"Laconella", gold ring with a thin line of platinum set with a "Spirit Sun" diamond*

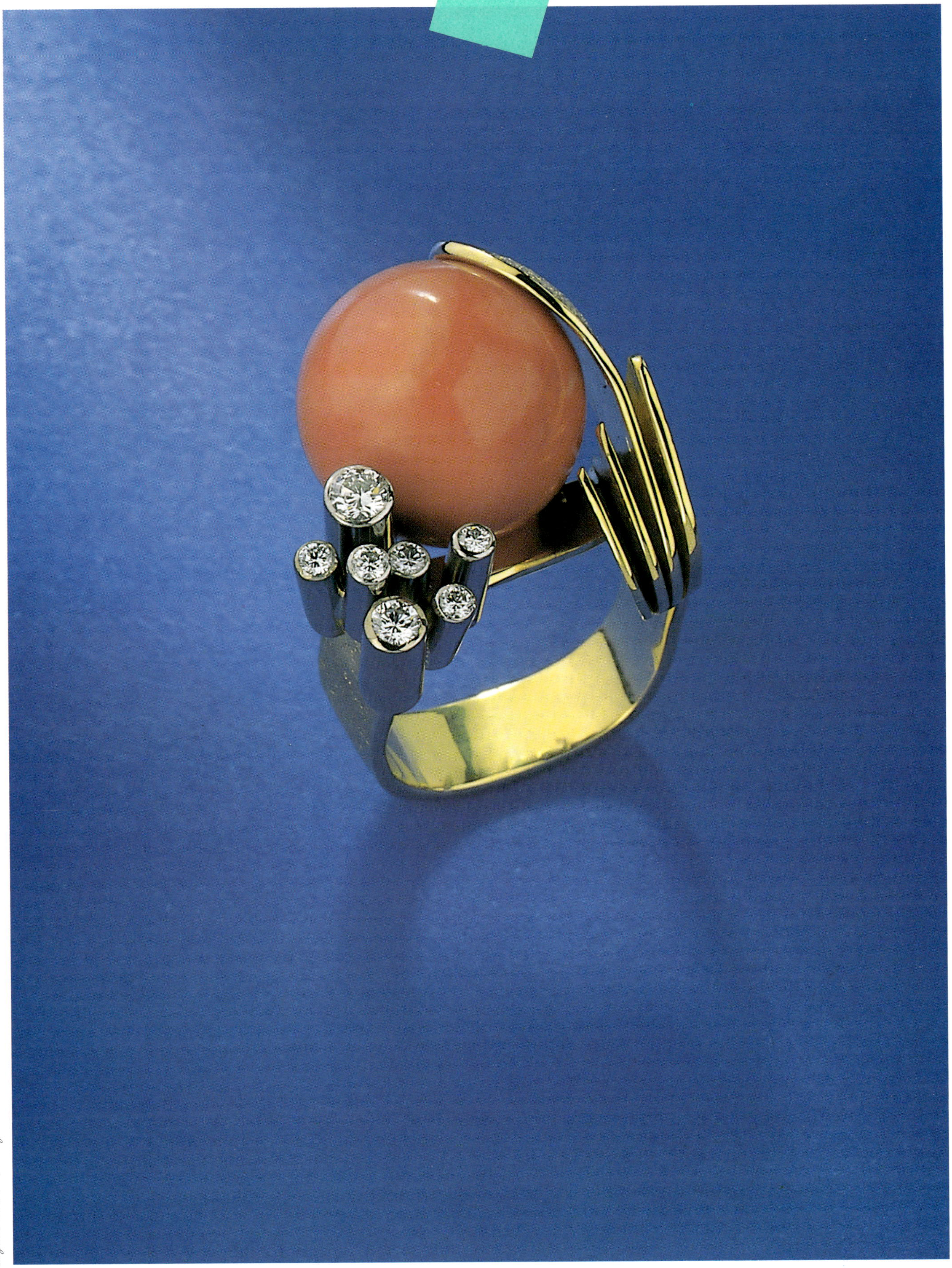

GREGOR TELGMANN, *"Geburt einer neuen Jahreszeit" ("The arrival of a new season"), ring.*
The fragile red coral is surrounded by protective gold. The diamonds descend from the sky like dewdrops to herald the end of winter, creating the effect of a sparkling firework

GREGOR TELGMANN, *"Sonnenreflexion" ("Sun Reflect"), ring in gold, platinum and diamonds. These two diamonds shine with their full brightness. "Spirit Sun" sends shining rays towards the earth; and so the earth is illuminated by the burning light of the sun*

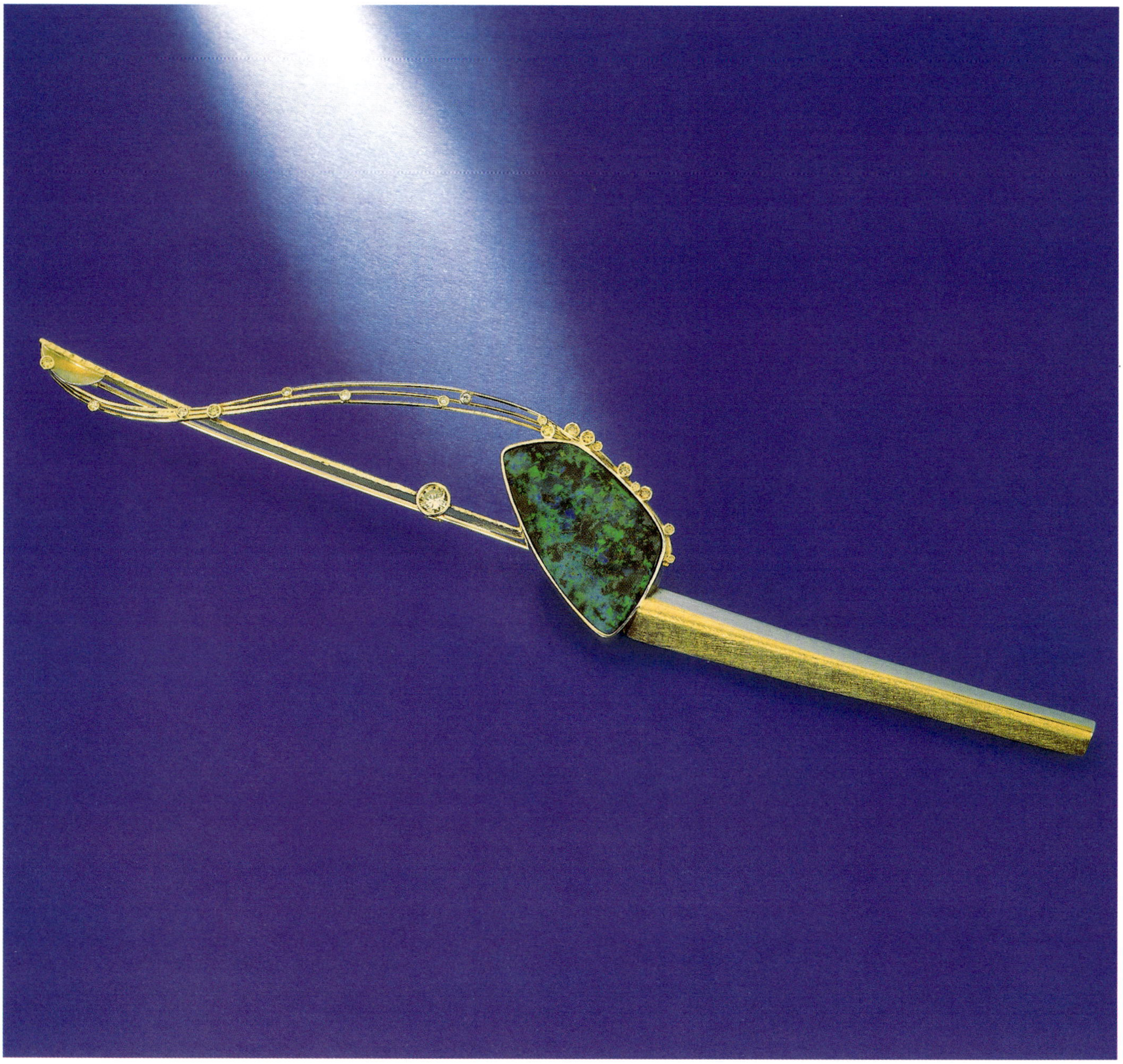

GREGOR TELGMANN, *"Im Garten Eden" ("In Paradise"), brooch.*
The brooch in smooth opal suggests man's joy at the idea of paradise.
Gold, platinum and diamonds point the way to this marvelous Eden

▸

GREGOR TELGMANN, *"Expérience fascinante des élements" ("Fascinating experience of the elements") sculpture. Joint work by Gregor and Alexandra Telgmann. Design by Gregor Telgmann. Sculpture made up of oil painting and jewelry with citrine. This artistic realization of an idea contains feeling and intensity. The cut citrine representing the sun ("Spirit Sun") portrays the elementary power of the sun. Man is resplendent in the brilliant sunlight, and experiences a new, fascinating world*

▲ TEREZA XAVIER, *"Brazilian Flag" collection. Bikini, hip jewel, bracelets, rings, in gold, rope made by the Indians and multicolored stones*

◄ TEREZA XAVIER, *bracelet in gold and diamonds, made using treated leather produced by the South American Indians. Designer Forum 97, winning collection. Gold solitaire necklace. Rings in gold and colored diamonds*

► TEREZA XAVIER, *bracelet/necklace/belt set with 57 brilliants weighing 11.50 carats*

KRISTA *and* GRETY VANDEVELDE, *"Dialogue".*
The Vandevelde sisters have been inspired by the natural form of these pearls. The symbol of duality finds expression in a triple dialogue between the silent discourse of the birds, the impossible fusion of the gold and the pearls and the intimate meeting of flesh and the material. Necklace in gold, brilliants and Keshi Tahiti pearls, winner of the first prize in the 1995/96 Design competition

KRISTA *and* GRETY VANDEVELDE, *two women create jewelry for women.*
The enthusiasm of the two sisters for jewelry has been aroused by precious natural materials, and through their art they have been able to discover the world and its bountiful treasures.
Grety elaborates precious materials for the joy it brings. She likes to amuse herself with jewels, to play around with pearl and to create a space of illusion for the eyes and the spirit.
For her, life is not serious.
Playfully it vacillates around circular, smooth and spiral forms.

KRISTA *and* GRETY VANDEVELDE, *"First flight", gold ring with green beryl and diamonds*

KRISTA *and* GRETY VANDEVELDE, *"Ebb and Flow", double-faceted necklace in gold, North sea shells and Tahiti pearls*

"Ebb and flow", detail

"The dialogue of the Vandevelde sisters". First, they must find the pearl, the one which speaks and which speaks to them. Then they must enter into dialogue with the pearl, allowing it to express itself, listening to it, studying its iridescent tones, drawing near to it in its round and baroque forms... They must allow it to seduce them, providing an appropriate resting place, its clothing of light.

KRISTA *and* GRETY VANDEVELDE, *"Spring tide", gold ring with North sea shell and Tahiti pearl*

KRISTA *and* GRETY VANDEVELDE

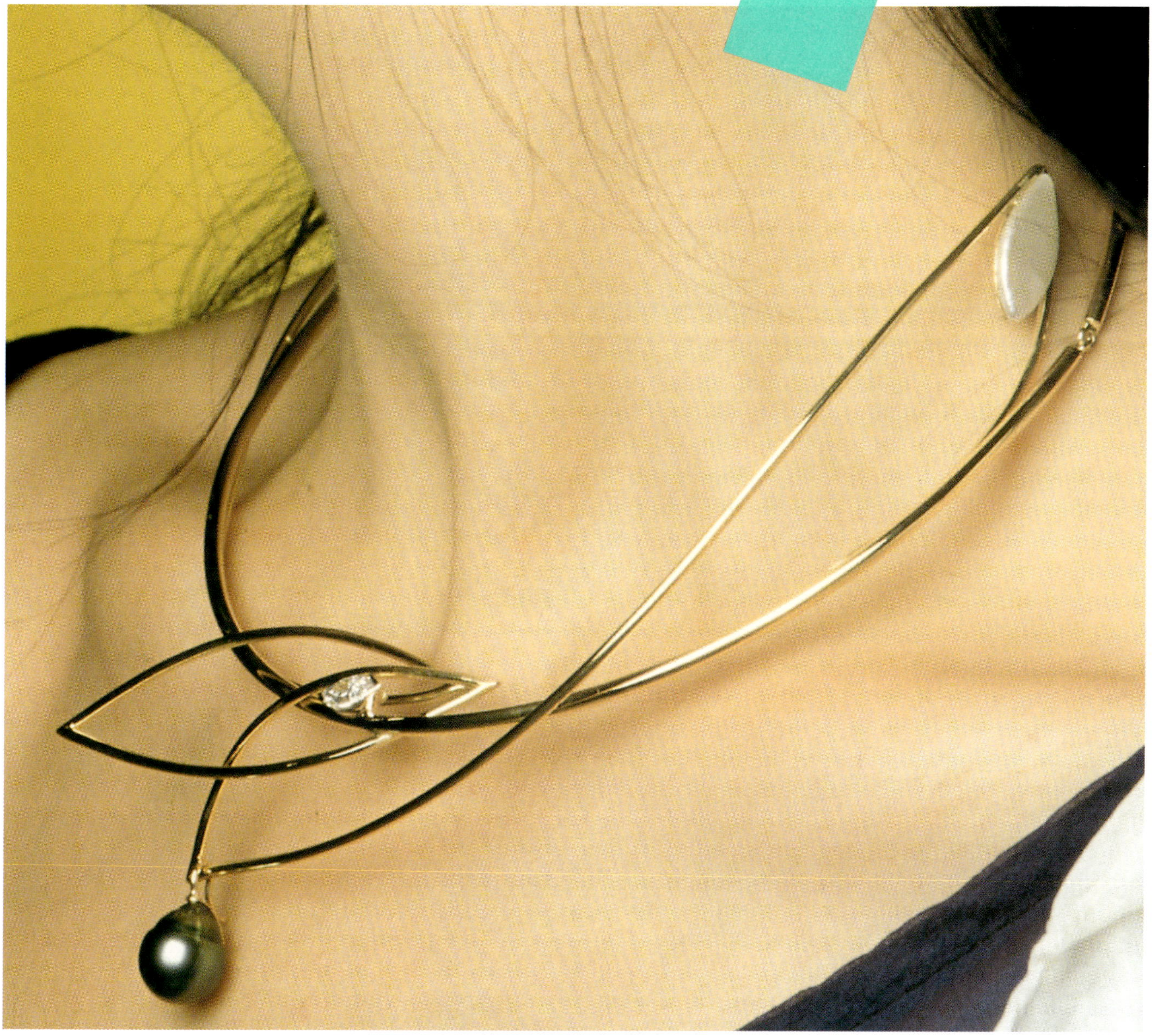

KRISTA *and* GRETY VANDEVELDE, *"Tango", necklace in gold, marquise cut diamond, Tahiti pearl and freshwater pearl*

She dances from form to form to make her dreams come true. Krista, her intuition always on the alert, comes close to the fusion of being and material. She searches out the initial source through her art. Her discoveries lead her to refine her spontaneous forms until she settles on the basic contour, the fluid energy. With a firm and rapid hand, she marks the pure and organic line that will reveal the unity of being. The strength of being a twosome. In two they give reciprocal support, in two they look, in two they progress, in two they select, take risks, inspire each other.
Krista and Grety create for the woman who will one day find herself in her jewels. Both make it a point of honor to wear their creations and to make jewels for each other, to give them to each other, to perpetuate the dialogue...

KRISTA *and* GRETY VANDEVELDE, *"Blizzard", gold ring with blue sapphire and "South Seas" pearl*

◂ SYLVIE LAMBERT, *"Intertwined with Gold", a superb transformable necklace. The central pendant reclines in wood, sanded or polished gold or gold set with pink or white diamonds. This timeless necklace is the test of love; and, like love, it continues to evolve over time. "Intertwined with Gold" is a line created by Sylvie Lambert for the modern woman.*

During the day it can be worn discretely without the pendant as a simple string of diamonds close to the face. In the evening the sparkling pendant is simply attached. Tomorrow it shall be the citrus wood pendant, and next month the pendant in carefully sanded gold.

WILLIAM GERMANI, *this bracelet in gold and precious stones can be transformed according to mood and tenor of dress*

▲ Nik Van Den Brande, *face ring in white gold and diamonds*

► Nik Van Den Brande, *breast ring in white gold and diamonds*

DANIELA BUFFAGNI, *"Paletta", brooch in gold, with leaves in agate, rubies and diamonds*

DANIELA BUFFAGNI, *"Angel", ring in gold, white and gray pearl*

VINCENT JAUMIN, *"Volute", sculpture in gold, lapis lazuli and elephant hair*

VINCENT JAUMIN, *"Destined", semi-pyramidal brooch in gold, rutile quartz and brilliants*

▲ THERESE SUDRE, *"Ligne Roseau"*,
"...far off the dragonflies hover over a garland of flowers coiled round a supple necklace in translucent resin."
These creations are all the work of Thérèse Sudre. They are original and refined jewels, full of poetry and harmony, in gold and diamonds ▸

Cathrine Clarke, *"Bamboo", earrings in green gold which offsets the color of the tourmalines. The whole is enhanced with diamonds*

ZARKHANE, *gold bracelet, a unique piece*

DANIELLE GOFFA, *conical gold ring. It picks up the reflection of three diamonds cut to appear in continual movement*

DONATELLA RIGHI FORTUNA, *necklace in Chinese coral, molten glass from Africa and Venice and jades set in 21 carats of gold. The Etruscan and Roman traditions are always present in Donatella Righi Fortuna's work. Her knowledge of precious and semi-precious stones, pearls, molten glass and antique coins is a determining factor in the decoration of her creations in 21 carat gold. The use of unusual materials and a specific style never prevents the artist from embracing new formal solutions which blend marvelously with the past. These pieces are one of a kind.*

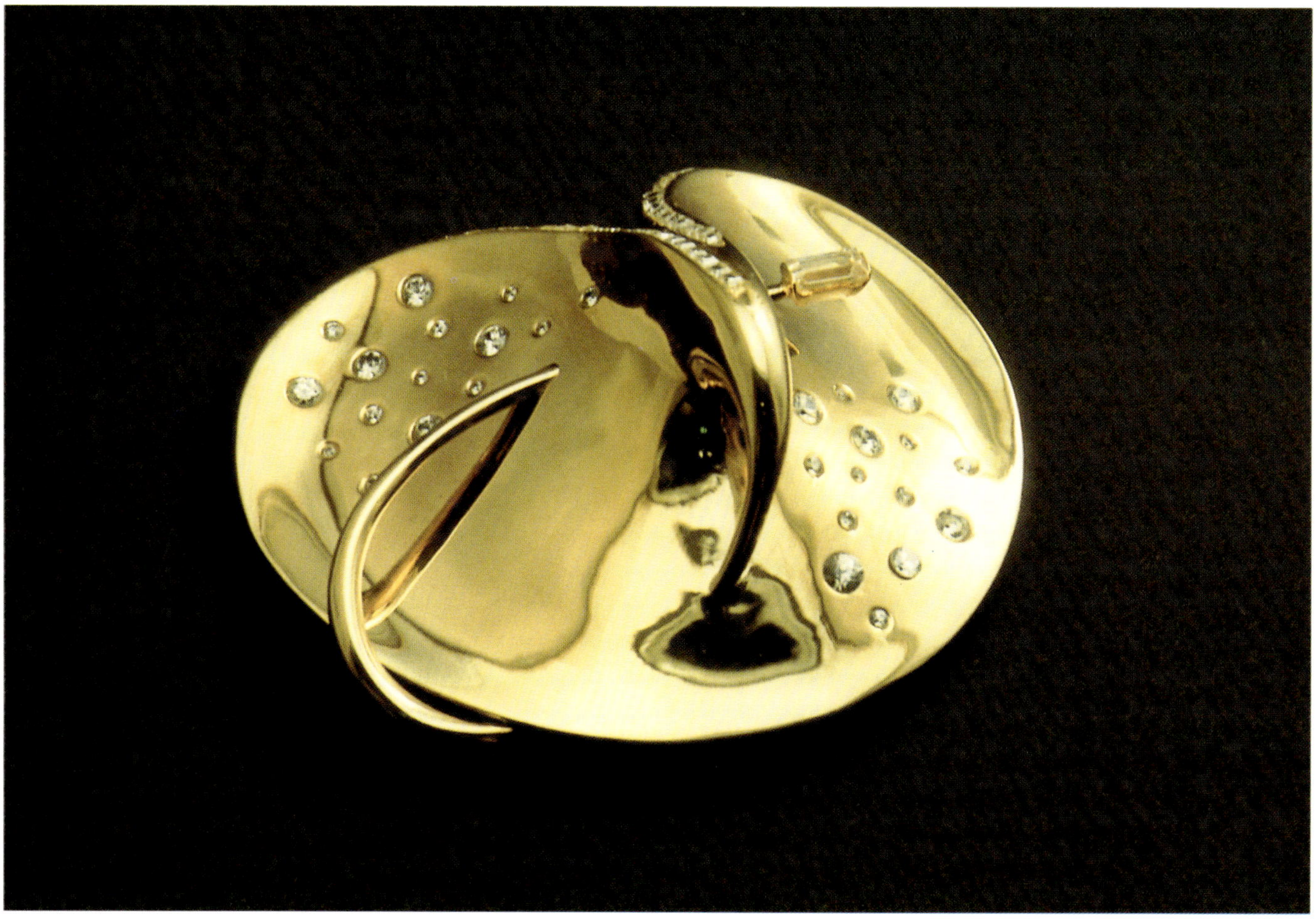

Patrick Lee

Anna Cella, *"Penelope", gold and silver bracelet*

ALBERTO ZORZI, *three brooches in gold, steel, soft agate and lapis lazuli*

ALICE HSIAO-YUAN LIN, *"Colors Symphony", pendant-brooch in white gold with green beryl, amethyst, garnet, and multicolored corundums*

SEGI, *"Creation of the night" necklace. The beautifully cut large purple amethyst set in the sharp, light 18 carat golden frame takes us in swirly purple rags to the mystical night. A night where only stars shed some light on the spectator (Diamonds)* ▸

SEGI, *creator of a multitude of forms, gives us a general survey of his numerous creations. Having made himself known through numerous exhibitions and publications alongside other famous artists, he also appears in the internationally-acclaimed work "The art of erotic jewelry", among the best designers in the world (Claude Mazloum). He has a particular love for minerals, 18 carat gold and diamonds, which he selects himself. Segi is renowned for his originality and for his interest in eroticism, the expression of which extends to his signature, a minute sperm. The works featured here carry us into the imaginary, sometimes dangerous, world of the artist*

SEGI, *"Segi", watch. If there is one eternal theme it is the theme of time. The triangle symbolizes the marriage of the earth and time. Materials such as gold and diamond reproduce the feeling of perenniality which time inspires. The tick-tock of the mechanism evokes a heart beat, the beating of the earth, on evey continent, in every universe*

Walid Akkad,
gold bracelet from the "Butterflies" collection

Walid Akkad,
brooch in gold and diamond from the "Butterflies" collection

WALID AKKAD, *necklace in gold and diamonds from the "Butterflies" collection*

WALID AKKAD, *brooch in gold and diamonds from the "Butterflies" collection*

PHILLIP MAYNARD, *necklace in sterling silver and cubic zirconium*

PHILLIP MAYNARD, *"The New Seed", pendant in silver and lapis lazuli*

ANGELO SPINELLI, *"HELBOP 1997", brooch created in honour of the passage of the comet of the same name. The creator hopes that this unique piece will still be fashionable at the time of the next approach, which is believed will take place sometime around the fourth millennium. In white gold, white and blue diamonds, and an arrangement of uncut stones at the heart (lapis lazuli, opal and angel hair), which portray the beginning of life at the moment of encountering another planet*

Jan Vanschoenwinkel, *necklace in gold and silk*

ALBERTO GIORGI, *"Golf", necklace in shining yellow gold and brilliants*

CHAPTER VI

Artist-Jewelers

In collaboration with ALBERTO GIORGI

Gold, Sun, Lion, King

by Mariano Apa

Beyond the profound darkness that emanates from the cave, the uterine mouth of the inverted mountain, the priest-magician patiently repeats the movements that produce gold filigree, open-work threads, anthropomorphic images that are printed on sheets with meticulous attention.

Possibly all that remains of these caves and these magicians is a slight trace, soon effaced by the water.

Of the fierce but gentle magicians that fashioned necklaces evoking a woman's scent, Cellini stands out in our memory; and it is congenial to read about his life in the depths of the night, when all the surrounding noises have finally ceased and the TV sets have been turned off, and it is possible to enter the world of these great Priests. In the nighttime silence he, like everyone that belongs to the corporation of goldsmiths, concentrates the intellect to build, hammer, forge, and ply the sacred metal, transforming it into the locus of perfection, the solid space between microcosm and macrocosm.

Patience, skill and the force of concentration combine with the idea to create the "jewel", a veritable stratification of meaning, a royal attribute, the symbol of solar rule, the rule of the King, the Sun, the Lion: iconographies of an ancient language in which the images could speak to all people to express the living Energy, the power of the spirit, the durability of the tradition able to turn lead into gold. From black to gold: the light of night is the light of day. In our secular century, should not the romantic aura surrounding the precious, enjoyed exclusively by those who work with gold, sustained by the concentration and strength of the idea, outlive the value of technique and skill?

Alberto Giorgi exemplifies this in his privileged experiences inside the *hortus conclusus* that forms a triangle with Fano, Pesaro and Urbino. It is a historical and geographical area where the memory of the equivalence between color and light, ideological and economic power is still alive. The painter Berruguete depicts Guidobaldo, the son of Federico, duke of Urbino, covered in pearls, amulets and jewels; similarly the "Baptist" in Piero's diptych shines with a pure radiance emanating not from a natural source, but rather from the gemstones, gold and silver that surround and describe the contours of his face, hair and neck.

The jewel is the expression of an ancient science that has assumed solid form as the microcosm of the inorganic unit, in order to mime the perfection, the wonder, the astonishment of being a jewel, or rather, of being a cosmic egg, a philosopher's gem.

Decorative jewelry is an adjective made from synthetic gold. The jewel that identifies with the self is the resplendent gold of the self: spiritual person, hero, knight, lady all at once.

Giorgi's jewels are not just decorative; they are an essential and lasting component of the psychology of the wearer. He does not consider a jewel to be in any way superfluous. It is a sign of psycho-cultural identity, of nobility, since nobility is the science that interprets the silence, the patience, the technique, the strength, the culture, the tradition, the recurring idea, necessary for the reproduction of the meaning and value of the macrocosm in the microcosm.

From necklaces to brooches, pendants to earrings or buckles, the piece of jewelry is made from white and yellow metal, colored stone, red and blue thread. Worn by men and women, the jewel is the identity that encompasses male and female, the microcosm and the macrocosm. It invites you to look for the Androgen.

Giorgi appropriates this ancient tradition, stretching from medieval and humanist corporations to the first family-run industrial initiatives and techno-scientific innovations, which has carried jewelry through the centuries, resisting market force, finally to become the privileged locus of contemplation, marvel, surprise. Contemplation of the rational idea that underlies the jewel. Marvel at the mastery of execution. Surprise at the beauty that manages to yoke intellect and poetry in the hardness of the stone, the tenderness of the forged metal, the specific quality of gold, the sign of the presence of the Light that shines in the dark of the Universe. These qualities, these "ancient" conditions live on in Giorgi's works; but he manages to translate the structural conditions of this ancient tradition into the stylistic language and burning critique of today.

Starting with Mannucci's teaching and the stylistic requirement that the burning center of the incandescent metal is represented in the shine of the stones that it contains, Giorgi has directed his search according to a constructive and dynamic logic, concentrating in the microcosm of the jewel the total energy of the forces able to rupture right angles and full curves. He brings together lines and geometrical figures that in turn give birth to a new geometry of space.

This geometrical organization of space is not, however, static and cold, with banal symmetries and volumetric relationships in formal equilibrium.

On the contrary, Giorgi develops intersecting and intermingling forms to create a geometry that follows the rules, but also the passion of feeling, the rush of intuition, the savor of poetry, a precious sonnet and true grammatical structure that speaks and dialogues.

In this stylistic context Giorgi elegantly transposes jewelry into sculpture and sculpture into jewelry. The narrow line - initially flat - broadens out and rises up, hardening to form a solid mass in space. Solid mass and transparent space: the essential components that transform the piece of jewelry into a sculpture.

In volumetric construction, Giorgi privileges the use of interlocking shapes with slightly mobile elements to edify the law of the machine. A machine that is "single" in the alchemical meaning of the word. A single machine that generates surprise at its conception, emotion and beauty.

The two-dimensional jewel and the volumetric jewel differ anthropomorphically and zoomorphically.

Ancient iconography taken from bas-reliefs in Roman churches and from the medieval imagination is here recomposed and reinterpreted through the geometrical organization of the iconographies and their consequent transformation into "single" iconographies; Giorgi manages to conceptualize and abstract even those iconographies

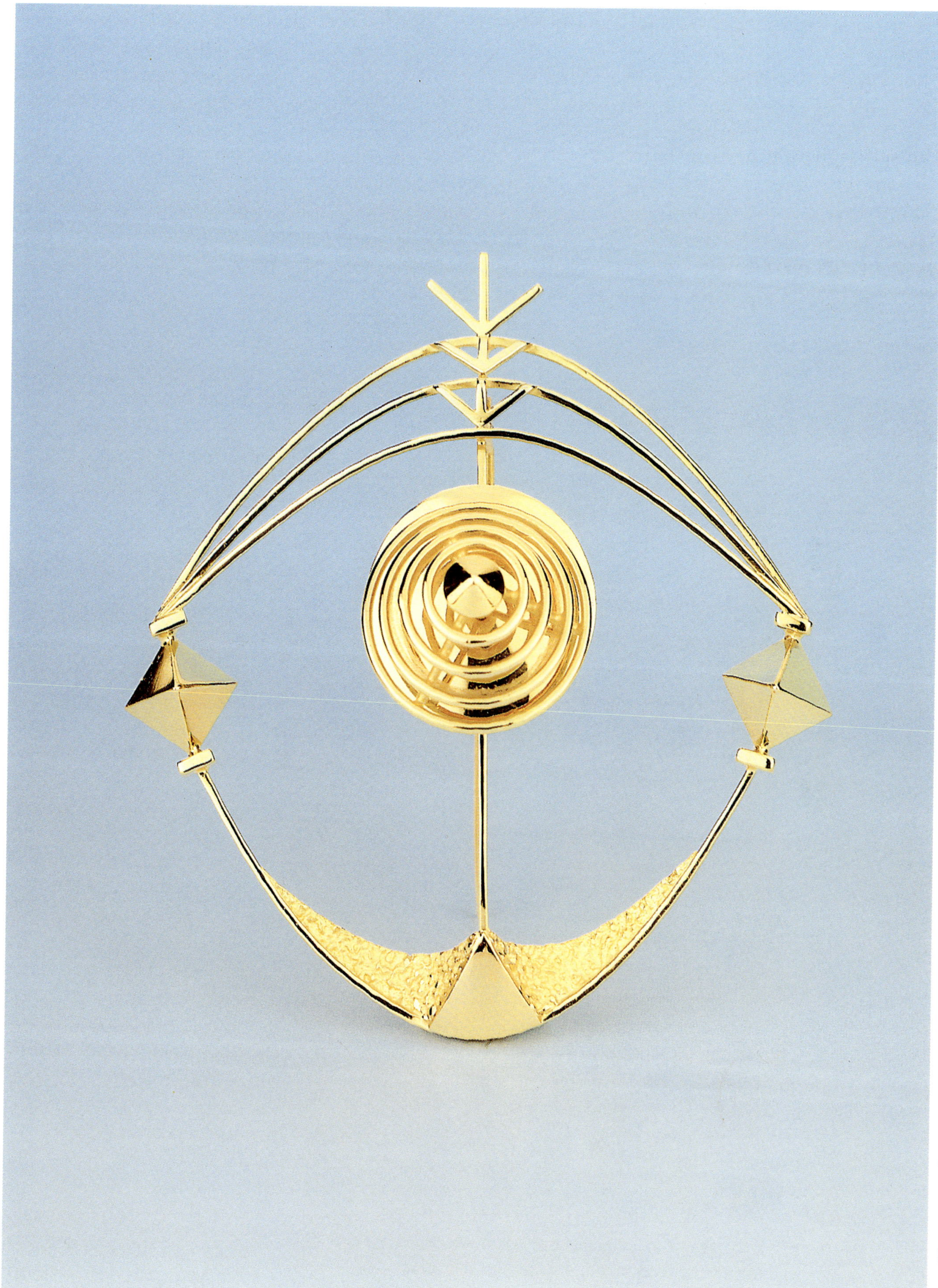

ALBERTO GIORGI, *"Arc", gold clip*

that contain references to Nature and History.

Giorgi's sculpture-jewels are "specula" images, "specula writings" representing everything and nothing, the entire solid and the empty outline.

The moving parts are like mobiles, giving the impression that the air, wind and nature have invaded an otherwise static mechanism.

It seems as though Giorgi means to give his geometric forms electric shocks, as though, like the ancient master goldsmiths, he wants to become a magician and priest of the ancient rite of forging an idea out of fire, concretizing it and transforming it into gold.

Spatio-dynamic research opens the door onto the modern world of today and tomorrow, in such a way as to project the ancient tradition into the future.

ALBERTO GIORGI, *specula gold ring with movable parts*

ANDREA GALASSINI, *brooches from the series "Animalia" in white gold and diamonds*

▲ KYRIAKOS SOMOS, *four gold brooches with American pearls and emeralds*

▶

KYRIAKOS SOMOS, *brooch-pendant in gold with 13.43 carats of citrine, 6.36 carats of tanzanites, 0.97 carat of tsavorites and 4.33 carats of tourmalines. Double pendant in gold with 2.54 carats of emeralds, 16.83 carats of black opals, 1.87 carats of tanzanites, and "South Sea" pearls measuring 10.5 mm in diameter*

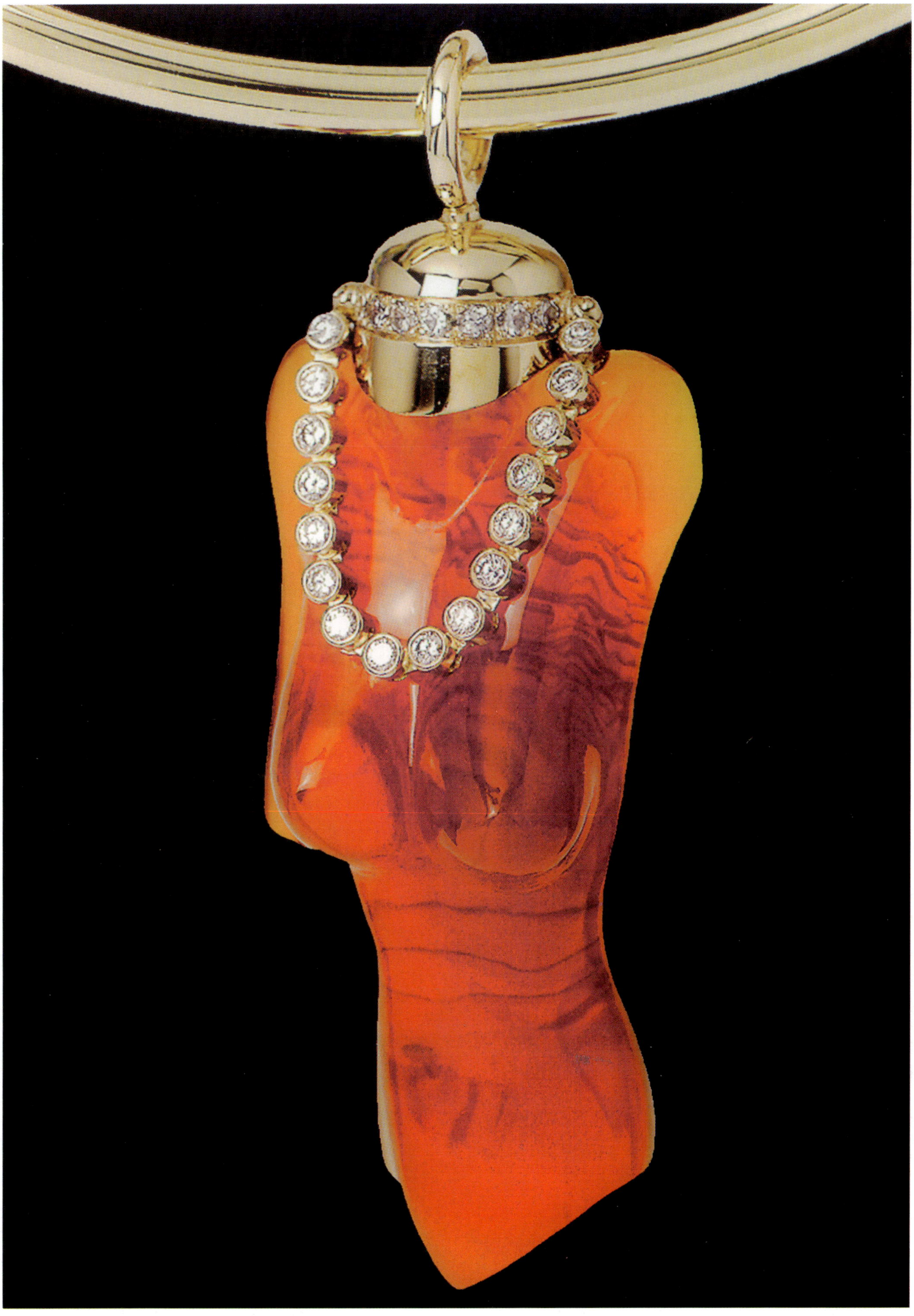

Stefan Pauli

Stefan Pauli

CHAPTER VII

Sculptors' Jewels

In collaboration with ANTONINO RANDO

All expressive forms and works of art have intrinsic value, by virtue of the fact that they are the fruit of the research and creativity of an artist.

This is especially true in the application of sculptural art to jewelry: the infinite potential of a metal like gold, best used on its own, is exploited to the full, not by the goldsmith or designer, but by the artist, the sculptor.

In this case, to create a piece of jewelry does not mean simply to conceive it and draw it, giving life to a decorative "object" that draws attention to its own preciousness. Instead, and most importantly, it means to give shape to an expressive form, independently of a result that must necessarily satisfy public and commercial demands.

This is the fundamental difference between a normal jewel and a "sculpture-jewel". The first is conceived to please, to attract, to seduce, often simply to satisfy cravings for luxury. The second is the result of a creative and expressive talent that transcends the boundaries of fashion, is not subject to external influences, but instead presents its own original language.

The application of sculpture to jewelry is rooted in history, although the specifics have been so unique and particular that it has been impossible to consider it as an art in itself, with its own evolutionary history.

What is meant by this is simply that sculpture has been applied to jewelry in different forms, in different ways, to different ends, and at different moments in the history of art; but it has always involved the symbiosis between the artist who creates and designs the piece of jewelry, and the artisan or goldsmith who elaborates and produces it.

This concept of the sculpture-jewel is still around today and produces admirable results. However, it is no match for the phenomenon that is commonly called "direct" application, according to which the sculptor or artist acts directly upon the precious metal without any kind of intermediary.

In my case, jewels come to life autonomously as works of art, having been conceived, designed and created as such.

The sculptor-goldsmith takes exclusive control of the entire production phase – the responsibility of the artisan – from research to elaboration. From the first wax models to the casting in gold to the mounting and polishing, the piece of jewelry is subject to elaboration and creative and manual modification by the creator until it assumes the expressive form that satisfies the needs of the artist himself.

This does not mean that the sculptor, by using a material like gold, which is so different from the more familiar wood, marble and bronze, restricts himself to the formal interpretation of his own expressive desire; he also tries to create "useful" forms that are balanced and "wearable".

Notwithstanding the preciousness of this material, the artist must do more than simply observe its intrinsic value; in fact he must

ANTONINO RANDO, *"Life", watch-sculpture in gold and crocodile skin*

obtain an appropriate balance of technical mastery, workmanship, taste and creative talent.

This is crucial for obvious reasons. Jewelry – the subject under consideration – must also meet the demands of the person choosing the sculpture-jewel to appropriate a message and present it – a message which from that moment is nothing other than the synthesis between the artist and the person wearing his piece.

It is in this very delicate transfer that the sculpture-jewel emerges as a pure and simple work of art, no different from any other unique expressive form and totally untouched by the rules of an industrial market that increasingly reacts to public demand alone.

This is the origin of a piece of jewelry that transcends the idea of beauty to gradually become part of us and of our daily emotional reality.

ANTONINO RANDO, *"Immersion", gold necklace. This thread of splendid Australian pearls symbolizes the birth of Australia with an imposing human and aquatic silhouette. An opal on the tail represents Australia's rich and precious subsoil and a lovely Tahiti pearl completes the natural beauty of the region*

STEFAN PAULI, *"Entfalte Dich", gold sculpture weighing 500 g*

STEFAN PAULI, *jewel-sculptures in gold and pearls*

STEFAN PAULI, *brooch-pendant in gold, lapis lazuli and diamond*

STEFAN PAULI, *brooch-pendant sculpture in gold and bronze with a diamond*

 HUBERT MINNEBO, *pendant, unique piece in gold and diamonds*

HUBERT MINNEBO, *pendant, unique piece in gold and diamonds*

SIMONNE MUYLAERT-HOFMAN, *necklace. This is a unique piece in gold, brilliants and opal*

CHAPTER VIII

The Color and Texture of Jewels

In collaboration with

SIMONNE MUYLAERT-HOFMAN

How pleasurable it is to look at these scintillating gold or silver objects, set with gemstones or pearls! Ladies eye them furtively, gentlemen dream of one day being able to give them to their beloved. Some of them really do shine with lustrous splendor, and admittedly this is reflected in the price. Out of the range of most people, every one of these pieces is a creation. Creativity in this context must be taken to mean the interaction of forms, the knowledge required to breathe life into the precious substance and sparkling gemstones. This is how Simonne Muylaert-Hofman sees it. She is a pleasant woman living in Nieuwstraat in Alost, for whom jewelry-making is a pleasure and a hobby, as well as a profession. Large or small, for all kinds of purposes; nothing is too difficult for her, although she admits that the outcome of her work is always uncertain.

Self-Taught

Strange though it may seem, Simonne Muylaert-Hofman has never been to school, nor had lessons or training in the jewelry trade, and especially not in the art of jewelry-making. Her talent is innate. As a child, she would spend her time at primary school making things. From this period, she displayed proof of her endless imagination. She often used to attract attention by appearing in clothes that she had made herself, dressed up with small pieces of jewelry made from glazed leather.

She remembers those years, in which she undoubtedly aroused a lot of interest, her imagination and her work guaranteeing her exhibitions at home and abroad. She continued for about 25 years, until one day she started to design jewels made from precious metals. This proved to be an excellent idea…

In fact, It is Sculpture

"Without further delay I set about collecting information about design, gemstones and the like, especially in Germany", says Simonne Muylaert-Hofman. "In fact, I am a sculptor. I use the lost-wax technique. First I design the jewel, and then I make it in wax. It is important that, once it has been cast, the piece appears in its definitive form, so that the stones can be positioned. A good imagination is required to do this, because at the design stage you need to plan the number and the position of the stones that you want to use. You must also know what to do with these stones, how to fix them. This is all very important when you are making jewelry."

"The following stage, in which the jewel is cast, is disassociated from the design stage. It is a technique, carried out by a skilled craftsman. In fact, once the jewel has been cast you have no more freedom. Of course, the design stage allows for continual changes: you can touch up the design, alter it until you get what you really want. I sometimes draw, or rather sketch a jewel that I have in mind. But I prefer to work in wax from the outset."

That was difficult

Simonne Muylaert-Hofman's pieces are often displayed in jewelry exhibitions. It is remarkable to note that she never seems to have to make an effort. She is always invited by people who believe in her creations, particularly because of their artificial spirit.

"It has not always been easy," she says. "When I think back over the last 25 years, I realize that I have come a long way, from artisan jewelry to my current creations. Now things are going well, and, you may be surprised to hear, my work is highly sought-after. Interest is not limited to particular social classes, either. Admittedly the price can sometimes be a problem, but I want to stress that it is not just rich people who buy my jewels. You would be surprised to know just how keen young people are to have a really "unique" piece of jewelry. I am all the more aware of this because I too was once twenty and wanted to have lovely things. I do not intend to make the creation of costly jewels my priority. I also create modest ones that young people can afford. And the attraction probably lies in the fact that every piece of jewelry is personal in some way."

They do not go out of fashion

Talking to Simonne Muylaert-Hofman is pleasant. She converses openly and knows her subject well. Here is what she has to say about the wearability of her jewels: "You buy them as you would a small work of art. They are as easy to wear as any other piece of jewelry. They do not go out of fashion, since jewels that are 25 years old are as beautiful today as they were when they were made. Of course, tastes can change, and a small alteration might be necessary. Sometimes long chains are all the rage, and sometimes short chains are in, but the jewel itself is timeless."

She is wearing a splendid piece, extremely costly, that does not get in the way when she goes out. "It is important to wear a jewel in such a way that it does not attract attention. In any case, when you go out it is usually hidden beneath a coat. Most people only notice large jewels, when in fact the smallest jewels are just as beautiful and distinguished."

Not enough time

Large or small, a piece of jewelry signed by Simonne Muylaert-Hofman is undeniably a magnificent specimen, unique and full of character. It is a living being, so to speak. The design reflects the tenderness of a female hand. Such a creative person as this has only one problem.

"I need much more time if I want to increase my output", she says. "Besides, I hate series work, and you will never catch me

SIMONNE MUYLAERT-HOFMAN, *brooch, a unique piece in gold, brilliants and sapphire*

 SIMONNE MUYLAERT-HOFMAN, *brooch, a unique piece in gold and Tahiti pearl*

SIMONNE MUYLAERT-HOFMAN, *brooch, a unique piece in gold and brilliants*

doing it. Every piece of jewelry is unique and complete in itself. I wouldn't want it to be otherwise."

If ever you are out walking along Nieuwstraat in Alost late one evening and you notice a small light burning in the back of a shop, do not think that it has been left on by mistake. You can be sure that a pair of artist's hands are in the process of creating a piece of jewelry bearing the signature of Simonne Muylaert-Hofman.

Published in *Het Laatste Nieuws*, 1989

"The flowers in Simonne Muylaert-Hofman's gardens are poisonous. They provide an irresistible reminder of the luxurious orchid gardens in Singapore, and give the impression of having been touched by the evil golden wand, by a kind of Hieronymus Bosch of jewelry: lunatic, unpredictable and, let's say it, a little bit disturbing.

The design of these pendants, brooches and bracelets seems, at first sight, to be disassociated from any geometrical pattern, to defy any clearly defined law of composition.

The artist, self-taught, certainly has an

easy and dexterous command of the techniques of jewelry-making, mastered through continual effort. The freedom granted by the lost-wax technique at the design stage is undoubtedly great. But it is right to ask how she uses this freedom, and to what end.

This question becomes increasingly important if we attempt to consider her work in terms of the exemplariness of its endlessly imaginative natural forms, the source of unanimous praise. But the interrogative remains, since the burgeoning of nature never occurs without a specific reason, which it is for the human intellect then to apprehend. In reality, Simonne Muylaert-Hofman always creates her pieces of jewelry around a gemstone or a rare pearl, taking this as her starting point. Two strangely opposing and contradictory directions are apparent in the artist's work. These directions can be seen individually and simultaneously, but their simultaneous presence always results in conflict, exploited with unfailing assurance. Agate, opal, ruby, tourmaline and all other precious and semi-precious stones naturally attract attention; and the relatively irregular force paradoxically tends towards regularity and geometric perfection, in accordance with the laws of physics governing the particular material.

In this case, the artist will invariably set the precisely-shaped gemstone in gold and a ring of brilliants to accentuate the very thing which prevents it from achieving its natural perfection. Thus she creates a balance based paradoxically on the imbalance from which it derives.

She finds the charms of mother-of-pearl even more exciting; and when the pearl is almost perfectly spherical, the gold, platinum and diamond corollary making up the piece of jewelry induces a state of delirium similar to the delirium generated by medieval Flemish paintings.

But Simonne Muylaert-Hofman is most fascinated by pearls presenting unpredictable shapes and unexpected colors; and she marvels at the diabolic parasites that are responsible for these fabulous, iridescent concretions with forms that are deeply disturbed, almost monstrous.

It is here that Simonne Muylaert-Hofman's talent reaches its peak. She forces the precious metal to exalt the basic deformity of the mother-of-pearl. She clasps the monstrous pearl in the golden tentacles of the jewel, slipping her diamonds into the intimate and painful folds that the mollusk has been made to produce.

Every piece of jewelry produced by this artist is a fossilized call, a method of making contact with the living heart of the material.

From a text by ALBERT BONTRIDDER

SIMONNE MUYLAERT-HOFMAN, *brooch, a unique piece in gold, agate and brilliants*

BATIA WANG,
"Sensuale"
("Sensuous"),
set in yellow gold

BATIA WANG,
"Landscape", gold brooch,
acrylics and rough
diamonds.
This object comes from
the "Dunes" collection,
representing sand dunes,
the sea and the sky

Atelier Siegl 1880

Hand-crafted in the Atelier Siegl 1880, these three original signed masterpieces demonstrate the different means of coloring and treating precious metal.

"YEAR 2000" by Jean-Marc Siegl. The shining setting in polished green gold edged with smooth platinum contains drop pearls in crimson red gold.

Roger Siegl has drawn inspiration for "FLOWERING" from Emile Gallé, adapting the techniques invented for glass by the Master from Nantes to traditional yellow gold, intense red gold, tender green gold and platinum, modelling these using a blowlamp to hold and enhance a ruby inlay with a singular cut.

"FIRE" is one of the jewels created by Elisabeth Borrani to represent the four indispensable elements for the artist in glass; the others are water, air and earth.
Here the fierce red, polished gold of the leaping flames contrasts with the cool yellow gold of the face.

An emerald carved on both facets to represent Christ's head is set against a silky yellow background.

The obverse with its chiseled pink gold cartouches commemorates the birth of Jesus and the sides display Christian symbols in yellow repercé gold.

The three signatures are inscribed in bright white gold.

The clasp label "BIJ'ART" also appears in the photograph (arrangement of model and label by Jean-Marc Siegl).

MICHAEL ZOBEL, *bracelet in gold, silver and jade*

MICHAEL ZOBEL, *brooch-pendant in gold and Australian opal weighing 11.50 carats and Keshi pearls*

CHAPTER IX

Message-Jewels

In collaboration with AGATHE SAINT-GIRONS

The beauty of a declaration,
the freedom of an expression

Jewelry has always been a mouthpiece for man and his feelings, whether to declare his love, reward and honor his courage, or affirm his social position or membership of a group. Just like flowers, jewels have the special gift of enhancing life through (self) gratification.

◂ AGATHE SAINT-GIRONS, *"Vive la vie", first prize in the international Ros Okabal Alcatel Bersil competition (1997). This piece was sponsored by Didier Guérin. Gold, 161 sliding precious stones, 30 star cut set diamonds*

AGATHE SAINT-GIRONS, *piece No. 28 in the exhibition "Love Potion", in silver and gold thread* ▾

Jewelry has always been a feature of human existence, from birth to death, eternally linked to religious and pagan rites.

The message-jewel both contains and is contained: it harbors a word, a treasure, a poison, or else it is a seal, a signature, a mark, itself becoming a message.

Today, contemporary jewelry is not restricted to its proper function, and its sculptural, abstract or figurative forms allow for greater depth of meaning in the message conveyed.

Destined mainly for adults, the message-jewel is, however, none the less playful (the "tool-jewels" of Anne Fauteux from Canada), loving (the "heart-in-your-hand jewels" of Florence Lehmann from France) or poetic (the "handkerchief-jewels of Xavier Domenech from Spain).

For some artists, this has even become the preferred MEANS of liberation. This is the case for "love potion", an exhibition of work by Agathe Saint-Girons of France, entirely dedicated to message-jewels. Between 1996 and 1998 the integral text accompanying this exhibition on its international tour has been translated into English, Spanish and Japanese, to make it more accessible to enthusiasts of the "precious message".

In this text, every word or phrase in bold type refers to a different jewel in the exhibition:

Love Potion

This is the story of a woman who wants **to explore everything the world can offer in a single lifetime.**

This is the story of **a woman who loves a man and will love another, again.**

The story of a desire to live **the beautiful and colorful life she had always dreamt of.**

The heart alone remained, lost, between his broken ribs...

She has to leave now. Search for the sun, the lava that once flowed through her veins, **the life-stream leading to the secret.**

She has absorbed quantities of blood and patience in order to feel alive. This new start has cleansed her ego. No more habits; nothing owed and nothing owned...

She is alone again, but stronger than ever. And she leaves, as light as a feather, towards new faces, different words, other thoughts.

Passages...

A being without a soul: haphazardly filling everything with beauty.

Like thinking without writing.

Lives that intertwine but unwind, incapable of distinguishing what binds them together.

Obsessed with an ideal: **an imprisoned love. Expectation...**

And our children. How we love our children!

This man with the broken ribs kept on coming back...

A terrible noise grinds into her brain. Waking up to gray Paris. She feels happy, ready to set off on a long journey.

Journey, how familiar this word is to her.

She gets up, looks out at the day, drinks her special concoction. On the bottle is written:

"Love Potion"

The message carried by the piece of jewelry is no longer contained only in the moment of giving, therefore, but also in the spirit with which it is presented and in the thought behind it.

However, the message-jewel is not conceived with the sole aim of being explicit; each shape, material or color is perceived or interpreted differently by each individual. And the possible combinations are infinite...

The message is more open; it allows room for imagination, leaving the wearer to react and express this reaction freely.

There is no compulsory interpretation any more: the message-jewel has become modern.

AGATHE SAINT-GIRONS, *piece No.1 in the exhibition "Love Potion", in silver, wood and gold leaf*

AGATHE SAINT-GIRONS, *"Passion is damned", silver and gold pendant from the exhibition "Man-Woman"*

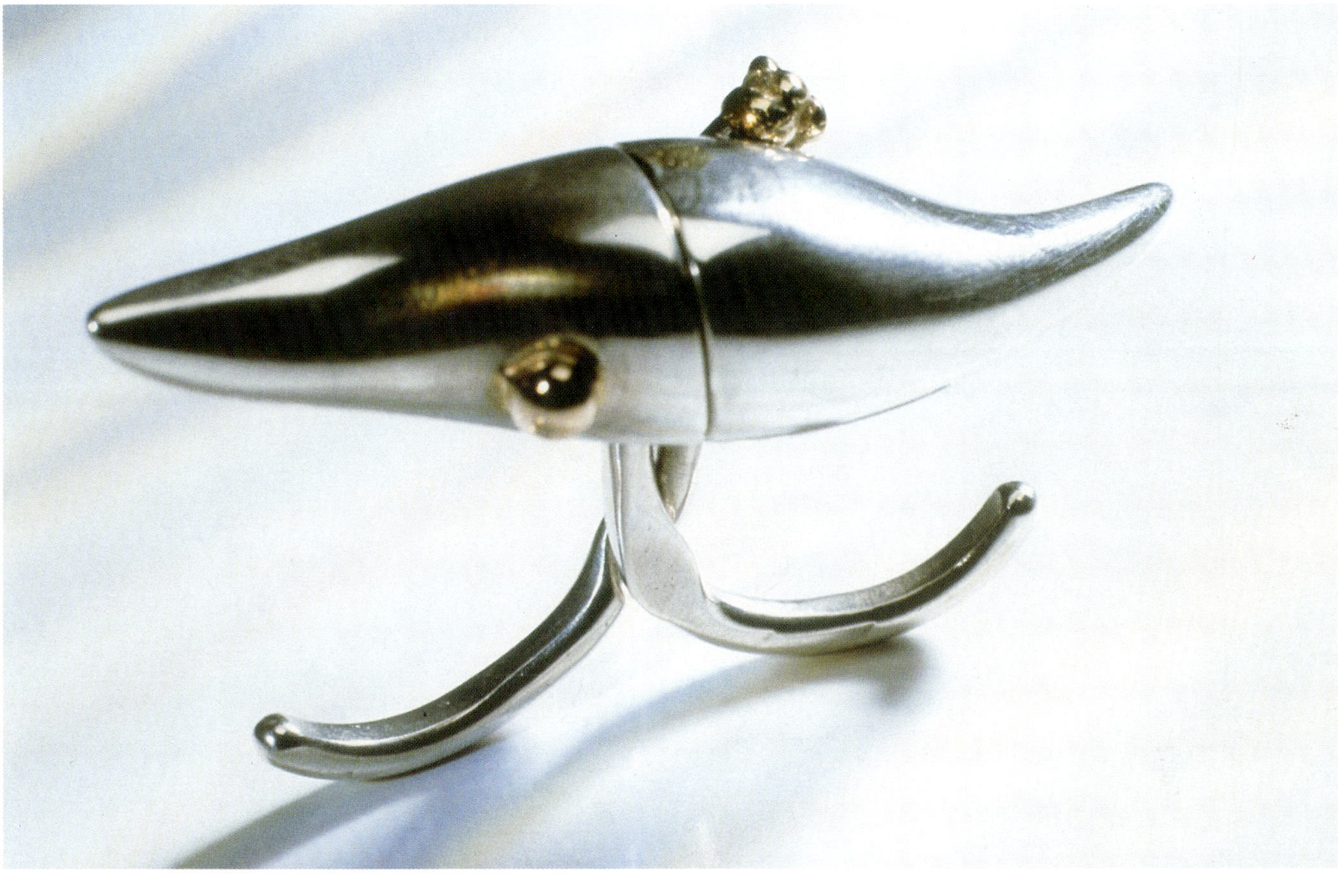

◂AGATHE SAINT-GIRONS, *"Traversée 4", pendant in ivory, gold and coral pearls from the exhibition "Love Potion"*

▴AGATHE SAINT-GIRONS, *"The life-stream leading to the secret", from the exhibition "Love Potion", in silver and gold*

AGATHE SAINT-GIRONS, *"Horny Ring", gold and silver ring from the exhibition "Man-Woman"*

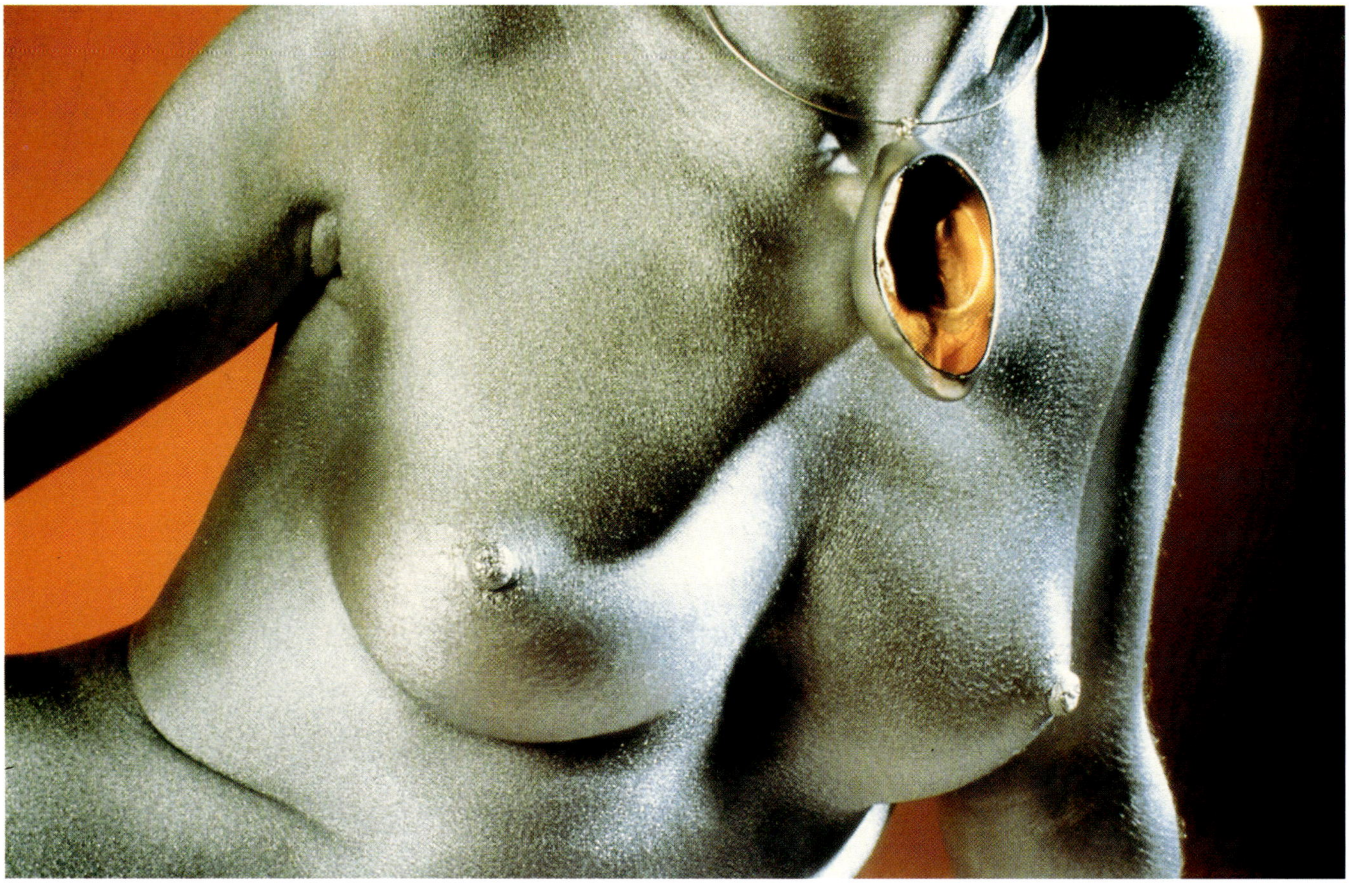

▲ AGATHE SAINT-GIRONS, *"Duals", silver and gold pendant from the exhibition "Man-Woman"*

FLORENCE LEHMANN, *"Cœur sur la main" ("Open-handed"), ring for the smallest finger of the left hand. Made of inlaid plexiglass*

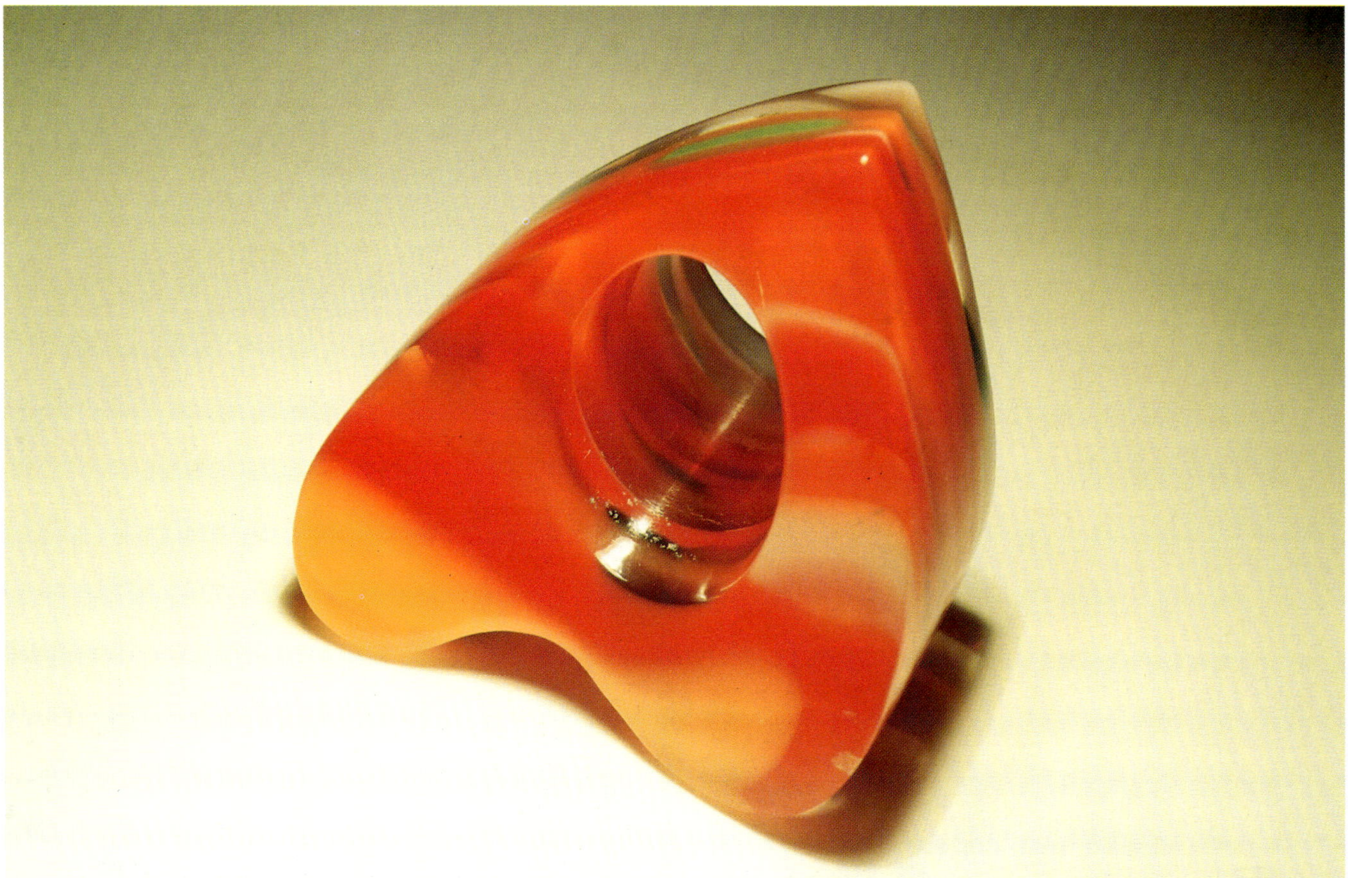

MICHAEL ZOBEL,
"Lippenring", gold ring with a natural brown brilliant of 0.38 carat and 25 cognac brilliants of 0.25 carat ▸

MICHAEL ZOBEL, *bracelet in gold, silver and coral* ▾

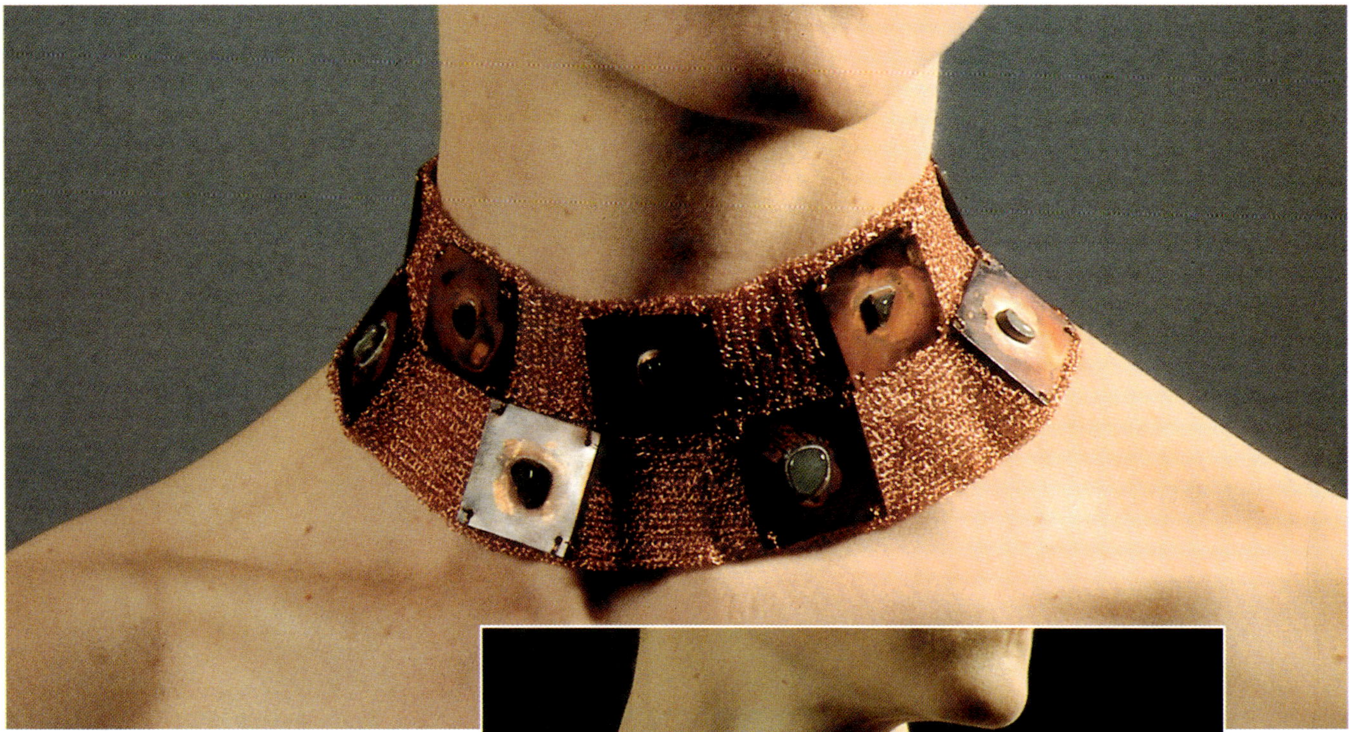

▲ Cornelia Freche, *multicolored necklace*

Cornelia Freche, *necklace "Unique Piece"* ▸

Cornelia Freche, *necklace*

PLATIN GILDE INTERNATIONAL

HANS SCHINDLER, *necklace and earrings in gold and platinum with "South Sea" pearls and diamonds*

CHAPTER X

The Return of Platinum

In collaboration with WILMA VIGANÒ

Platinum: the metal of the next millennium

Platinum enjoyed its boom for years, from the beginning of the century to the outbreak of the Second World War; it played an uncontested role in Art Deco jewelry. From 1939-40, it was requisitioned in the belligerent countries for military purposes because of its multiple industrial uses and strategic importance, and it disappeared from jewelry entirely.

After the war, major social changes took place. These were mirrored in the luxury goods trade, and the jewelry trade in particular. For a number of reasons (taste, fashion, decorative style, design, the spread of well-being and the diffusion of wealth), platinum was used almost exclusively in the production of luxury jewelry, that is, to create rare objects of great value, requiring the use of the most precious of precious metals.

Today platinum is staging a return throughout the world, thanks to the use of new mines and increasingly advanced techniques. It is characterized by the fact that it is more rare, and therefore more precious than gold, but at the same time more discreet. Elegant, pure, sober and modest, it is the perfect expression of the spirit of contemporary society and of the values upheld by mankind on the threshold of the new millennium. To acquire a piece of platinum jewelry for oneself or a loved one is to make a deliberate and rational choice, in an act of self-affirmation implying the search for originality and perfection.

The intrinsic qualities of platinum (nobility, incorruptibility, brightness, color) make it especially popular with young people, symbolizing as it does the eternity of love and the indissolubility of marriage. Thus the wedding ring and engagement rings were the first items to witness the return of platinum in jewelry, in Japan, the Far East and throughout the Western world.

Today, however, it is no longer a question merely of rings. Shiny or with a satin finish, white or with a color approaching gold, with or without stones, platinum has now established itself as a metal which, with its extraordinary ductility and manufacturability, offers the designer and the goldsmith the most satisfactory creative options.

This, the king of metals, triumphs in daring creations that are impossible in other precious metals; it defies the most established stylistic and technological rules; it moves forward with its characteristic indomitable force to explore new boundaries of avant-garde taste and design.

But platinum is sober, which is why in recent years it has become the preferred metal of the male public, who choose it for the most prestigious accessories, starting with watches. Now all the big names produce platinum-covered cases to protect the precious technical movements of the internal mechanism.

Platinum is particularly popular with young people.

In both the established markets in America, Europe and Japan, and in the newly-emerging markets in China, India and the Middle East, a new style of jewel made from platinum is appearing. Pure and simple. Easy to wear. Young and carefree. Precious but accessible.

A jewel that answers the needs of the new buyers, in search of simplicity, elegance and sobriety in an object that is symbolic, intimate and personal rather than indicative of status.

The world is currently experiencing a change in taste, in which the consumer is the demanding protagonist, in search of a lifestyle that is authentic and personal. With its unrivaled intrinsic and cultural characteristics, platinum would seem to provide the best answer to the demands of the new millennium.

SIMONA FAVILLA *and* MARCO MINELLI, *pectoral in platinum, rock-crystal and pastel crayons*

KOALA PREZIOSI, *necklace and bracelets in platinum and gold designed by Alberto Zorzi*

Platinum is...

...precious

Platinum is certainly the most precious of the precious metals. It is the most rare, the most pure, the most resistant, the most important, but also the hardest to manipulate (it offers unique expressive possibilities).

...mythical

Platinum is a myth. It was a myth in the 1920s, when it was used successfully to create the daring geometrical forms of Art Deco, intriguing Joplin and Ella Fitzgerald, Mary Pickford and Cole Porter, Greta Garbo and Jean Harlow, the famous "platinée". It had already been a myth for centuries before the Spanish conquistadors named it "platina", meaning "low-quality silver".

Roughly one hundred years before the birth of Jesus Christ, the South Americans liked to be seen wearing pieces of jewelry made from platinum and gold. The small coffer belonging to the Egyptian priestess Shepenoupet, decorated with pieces of platinum by a craftsman from Thebes, is over 2500 years old. Such is the force of this metal that it was deemed a suitable decoration for Agamemnon's armor, described by Homer in "The Iliad".

...rare

Platinum is exceptionally rare, and equally precious. According to calculations, if all the extracted platinum in the world was combined to form a single solid, it would make a cube measuring about 4.6 m.

Deposits of platinum are also rare. The richest deposits are located in South Africa, producing about 75% of the global output. Less significant deposits are also to be found in Russia, Canada, the United States and Zimbabwe.

Annual production amounts to around 120 tons compared with 2500 tons of gold. To obtain one ounce (3.1g) of platinum, it is necessary to extract and work 10 tons of rock. It takes five months of labor to get from the raw material to the ingot. To obtain the same quantity of gold, three tons of stone and between four and five weeks of labor are sufficient.

The effort is huge. But the result is a metal with unique qualities.

...unalterable

Weighing 21.45g per cubic centimeter, platinum is the heaviest of the precious metals. Twenty-four carat gold weighs 19.3g precisely, while pure silver weighs 10.5g. At 11.35g, lead is incorrectly considered to be the heaviest metal.

Moreover, platinum has a very high melting point: 1773°, compared with 1063° for gold and 960° for silver. Other characteristics combine to make it unique, such as its resistance to chemical and physical agents (it is unaffected by all acid and alkaline solutions, except for nitrogen sulfate at 70°) and its ability to withstand heat, for example.

Because of its intrinsic qualities, when the decimal system was adopted in 1795, the standard meter length and kilogram weight were made from platinum. They are still on display at the Pavillon de Breteuil in Sèvres, near Paris.

...strategic

Thanks to the same extraordinary characteristics, platinum is considered of real strategic importance, being used in the most advanced areas of industry, technology and science.

Platinum is so important that only 40% of global production can be used to make jewelry. It is used in the fields of medicine and chemistry, electronics and energy, petrol and glass. It is fundamental among other things in the manufacture of pacemakers, fertilizers, high-quality glass, glass fibers and cathode ray tubes.

The catalytic properties that it displays are used to reduce atmospheric pollution generated by vehicle exhaust fumes.

Platinum is also an excellent investment; about 7% of global production is conserved as ingots and coins.

...pure

The purity and amazing ductility of platinum make it ideal for jewelry manufacture. The pure metal content in the alloy used in jewelry is 950/1000; one gram of platinum generates a two kilometer thread.

Platinum is totally compatible with every type of skin, it neither changes nor erodes, it protects the precious inlays better than any other material, and its neutral color enhances their beauty without ever eclipsing their brightness or their color. The most famous stones in the English crown jewels, the Star of Africa and the Koh-i-Noor, are set in platinum.

Big-name jewelers like Cartier, Tiffany or Fabergé have always risen to the challenge presented by platinum to their technical skill and creativity. The most famous contemporary creators have followed suit. They apply themselves to the full exploitation of platinum in the search for a new design and a new relationship between man and jewelry.

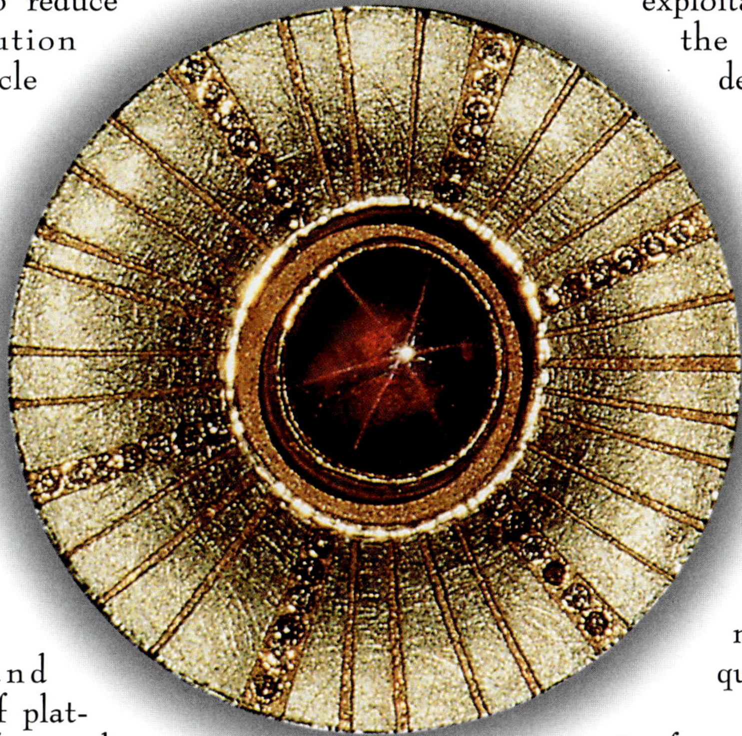

...distinguished

"Nothing but platinum is acceptable with evening dress", said the Duchess of Windsor, expert on jewelry and model of social etiquette.

In fact, in the evening, the moonlike reflections produced by platinum are particularly elegant, refined and seductive. However, the fascination of platinum is evidently general, and linked to all these "added values" that have made it into a myth and raised its preciousness above the level of its intrinsic value.

▲ MICHAEL ZOBEL, *ring in gold and platinum with a star ruby from Ceylon weighing 6.36 carats and 36 natural pink diamonds weighing 0.36 carat*

WOO HYUN CHOI, *"A Happy Day", necklace in gold, platinum, diamonds and Tahiti pearls*

MICHAEL ZOBEL, *bracelet in gold and platinum with rough and cut diamonds*

KURT SCHAFFO, *skeleton watch in gold and zirconium, made completely by hand*

CHAPTER XI

Artist-Watchmakers

In collaboration with

KURT and CHRISTOPHE SCHAFFO

In spite of the evolution in thought and technological progress, society is always going to produce élite groups, cultivating certain attitudes, including the love of beauty. Watchmaking does not escape this rule, and connoisseurs are not going to let up their search for prestigious signatures.

Of these signatures, Kurt Schaffo's is destined to survive. The artist modestly calls himself an artisan – he whose hands produce such marvelous "time-keepers"...

Like a monk in his cell in the peaceful Neufchâtel mountains, Kurt Schaffo patiently cuts and assembles the minuscule parts of a cunning mechanism. Running away from the series production that is so antithetical to his character, this man entered the "Order of the Ancients" over twenty years ago. Since then, he has dedicated himself to the cult of an ethic, to the rigor of an art whose masterpieces are carefully preserved in museums, such as the hand-made watch, a unique item. And the use of the word "watch" to describe such marvels suddenly seems rather indecent. There is need for a term better suited to the beauty of these fantastic creations.

Where do these "time-keepers" covered in gold, gemstones or brightly-colored enamel then end up? How much do they cost? Having played carefully with a couple of models, these are the questions that come to mind – embarrassing though they are. The man smiles and replies philosophically that enthusiasm alone is insufficient to cover his needs. Connoisseurs of all nationalities, sometimes traveling long distances, come to visit Kurt Schaffo in the village of Locle, formerly one of the birthplaces of the Swiss watchmaking industry. Collectors, or quite simply lovers of beauty and authenticity with a taste for originality, these visitors are able to express their particular desires regarding the sophistication of the mechanism and the decoration of the case. These will be granted as far as possible. Kurt Schaffo has passed on his ethic to his son, Christophe, who trained at the Chaux-de-Fonds Art School. Thanks to his artistic background, he has been able to master drawing, miniature and ultra-fine engraving quickly. Encouraged by his success at the "grands faiseurs" in Switzerland and abroad, Christophe has decided to devote his talents as stylist-designer to designer watchmaking. And so, for several years now, he has been designing and signing his own creations, as well as guaranteeing the finish displayed by his father's jewels. Now we can expect to see a new name appear in the watchmaking museums. It must be said finally that every model with the Schaffo signature is regulated with the utmost precision and accompanied by a certificate declaring its uniqueness.

"La Signature de G. Droz"

KURT SCHAFFO, *skeleton watch in gold and zirconium made entirely by hand; hand-wound woman's watch in platinum. Automatic man's watch in platinum*

KURT SCHAFFO, *pocket watch in gold, enamel and aquamarines, made entirely by hand*

CHRISTOPHE SCHAFFO, *gold, diamonds and leather*

CHRISTOPHE SCHAFFO, *watch in gold, diamonds and sapphires*

CHRISTOPHE SCHAFFO, *telling the time in gold, diamond and cork*

ROBERGE, *"Andromède II Dame". Case in pink gold, rounded sapphire glass, face in mother-of-pearl and rubies*

ROBERGE, *"Andromède II Dame". Case in pink gold, rounded sapphire glass, face in mother-of-pearl and diamonds*

ROBERGE, *"The Flaming Star". Case and bracelet in gold set with diamonds and baguette cut rubies. Electronic mechanism encased in 4.88 carats of diamond*

ROBERGE, *"Nymphéa". Watch-jewel.*
Unique piece in 18 carats of pink gold set with 514 pink, yellow and white diamonds weighing 65.54 carats in total.
The face is set with 40 baguette cut diamonds (2.21 carats), with a multi-faceted, rounded, anti-reflect sapphire glass cover.
Case and bracelet set with 229 pink baguette cut diamonds (5.45 carats), 167 yellow baguette cut diamonds (3.31 carats), 28 yellow round cut diamonds (1.78 carats), 24 white emerald cut diamonds (19.84 carats), 24 white round cut diamonds (29.91 carats), enhanced by two pink oval cut diamonds weighing 5.36 carats and 5.34 carats respectively

ROBERGE, *case and bracelet in gray gold set with baguette cut sapphires. Face set with brilliants*

ROBERGE, *case and bracelet in gray gold set with diamonds*

Christophe Claret, *"symbolic"*, watch-bracelet

▲ANTOINE PREZIUSO, *"The hours of love", watch*

▲ANTOINE PREZIUSO, *watch, reverse side (no explanation needed)*

ROBERGE, *"Andromède RS", chronography. Mechanic-electronic mechanism, anatomic steel case*

MARIA-GRAZIA DI GIANDOMENICO, *design for a pendant-flower-carrier in gold and diamonds*

CHAPTER XII

The Accessories of the Future

In collaboration with

MARIA-GRAZIA DI GIANDOMENICO

We used to equate the year 2000 with a revolution in taste, imagining ourselves clad in silver and flying inside high-tech space ships in orbit in far-away galaxies. Now, at the approach of the third millennium, we find ourselves looking backwards, not to see how we can use a period of history, but how we can copy it. In 1912 Boccioni underlined his thirst for renewal: "...the sculpture of every country is dominated by the blind and stupid formulae handed down from the past, imitation fueled by the double cowardice of tradition and ease..." But today large and small-scale producers find themselves trapped in the magnetic field generated by the monsters of the past.

What do we want men and women to be wearing in the twenty-first century? This question triggers new ideas for pieces of jewelry, multi-functional accessories, both cheap and expensive; they will be made from simple threads and sheets, without designs, decorations or colors, almost as though they were pieces of wearable rubbish.

In history, the same events are often repeated with different protagonists. Looking at the products of the modernist movements, the avant-garde, and thinking about the global reports, the arguments that consider decoration to be the death of art, the rejection of historical forms and elements, we find ourselves making the same mistakes as those who copied rather than creating.

The jewelry industry has not limited itself solely to the naïve decoration of commonly-used objects to make them beautiful as well as useful; it is decoration itself. By bedecking his hair with a hairpin, his coat with a brooch, his belt with a buckle, man allows himself to be directed by the same impulses that drive him to embellish a saucepan or other quotidian items.

In this century, art conforms to the different aesthetic, functional and ideological trends; it thrives on its contradictions. The jewelry of Cartier and Lalique originates in this idea of decoration, based as it is on the assemblage of antique pieces, or on inherently beautiful excavated remains. The jewelry of Fontana, Calder and Pomodoro, alternatively, is the formal transcription of their art. The history of jewelry is a labyrinth of excesses, abuses and the intelligent recovery of the major traditions. It is useful to conduct an end-of-the-millennium analysis of designer jewelry or precious accessories to see how these items have evolved, in order to progress and to produce new forms and ideas, looking at the past reverently but without copying it. The forces of history are admittedly slow; and so, although there were designers in the 16th century, it is only this century that renewal has been recognized, in an area of art history long neglected and overlooked and which has presented no real development for more than two centuries. People have always worn accessories, to complement their outfit or decorate their head or neck. However, these defensive tools have slowly evolved, becoming increasingly complex in decoration and design, satisfying the demand and the dream of wearing them. In Egypt, the ornament reached levels of refined beauty, becoming so important that everything was transformed into a precious accessory; every piece was covered in symbols figuring the protective divinities, gods whose role it was to guide in life or in the journey towards the river of the afterlife, and took on magical significance. Precious metals and gemstones have gradually abandoned their function as talisman, reaching a level of expression that is more mundane, such as to mark an important moment in the life of a couple. Jewels are characterized by durability, in a society that is enslaved by the ephemeral and by short-term commodities. In addition, they are top of the list of objects that serve pleasure, and have become one of the most important forms of decoration, carving for themselves an ever greater role, thanks of course to the creative talent of the artist.

Workmanship is involved in painting and sculpture as it is in other art forms, although paradoxically it is not the idea that is rewarded, as much as the finished product. Simultaneously, the precious accessory, still classified as designer jewelry or precious sculpture rather than simple art, is gaining ground as a "major" art form.

Of course, accessories are designed not according to need, but for pleasure. They can be perceived as fleeting thoughts that are subsequently translated into a project, designating men of reputation and pleasure – the pleasure of studying the material and simultaneously thinking of the artist who fashioned it.

What will be the needs of the future buyer?

What will the accessories of the future be like?

In the early years of this century, handbag fastenings transformed into earrings, bracelets would enclose a carefully hidden watch mechanism. We will continue to decorate our shoes with jewels, and these will probably be detachable and double as earrings or pendants.

All this brings to mind those mechanical children's toys, transformed in the capable hands and by the impetuous imagination of their young owner. What change will the powder-box or the perfume-bottle undergo to suit a woman that spends increasing amounts of time thinking and organizing? It would be easy to combine a pen and lipstick in the same object, or to relaunch the idea – reformulated – of a brooch or pendant that doubles as a container holding the perfume of a fresh flower: a container of essences too, that fulfills our actual need for perfume to re-evoke rites now distant in space and time.

The precious accessory will change in the same way that society will change, renewing itself along with the other arts that will finally no longer be classified in terms of greater or lesser importance, or primary and secondary value.

Art is directed by experiment; and the same must be true of the jewelry industry insofar as it embraces new materials that are assembled and rendered unique by virtue of an artistic conscience.

What will the jewel of the future be like?

It will be like the society of the future.

"Form is given significant collective value by the artist." (Enzo Mari).

MARIA-GRAZIA DI GIANDOMENICO, *design for a precious shoe*

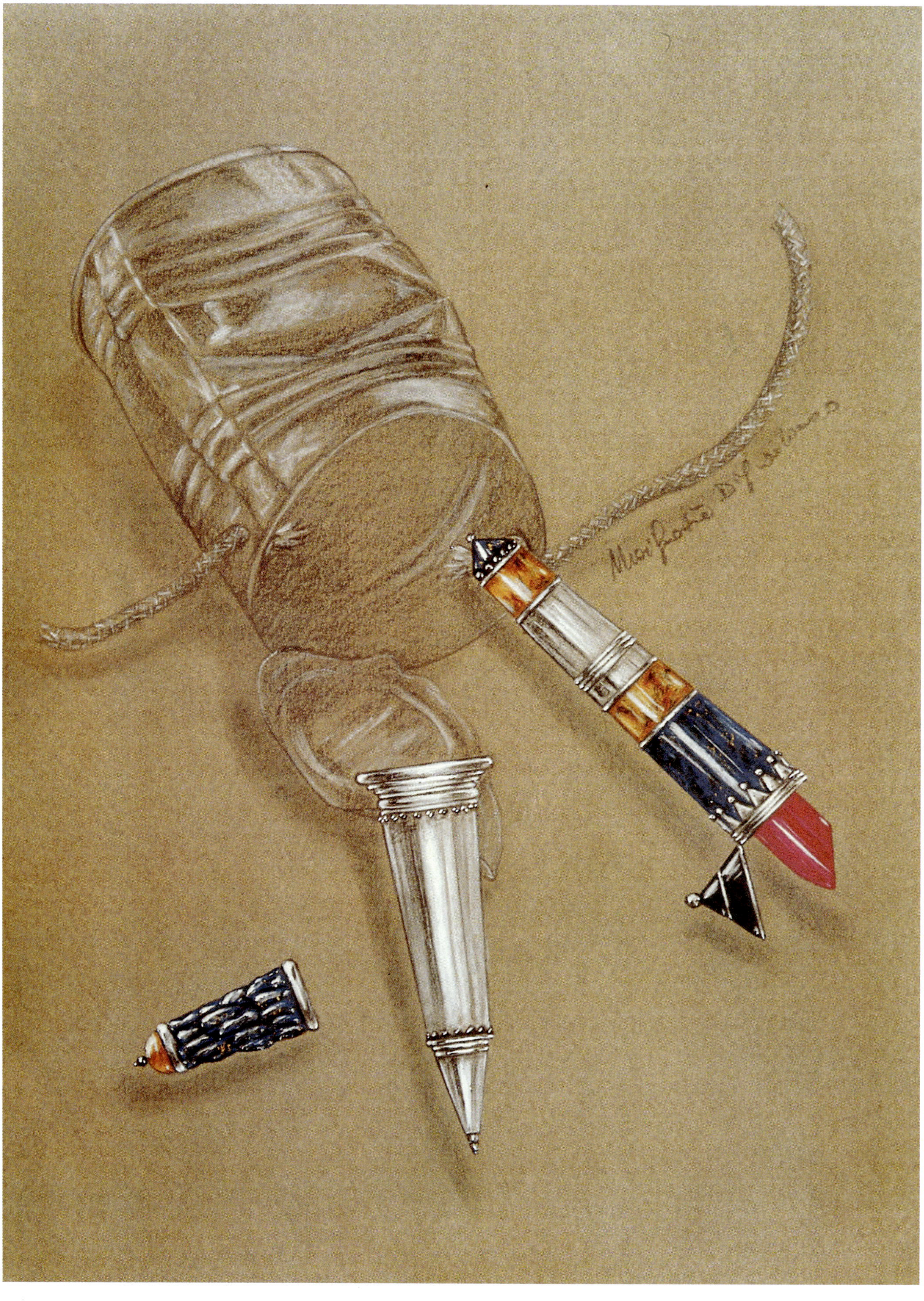

MARIA-GRAZIA DI GIANDOMENICO, *design for precious accessories*

Claude Mazloum, *"A man of great modesty, Claude Mazloum is an artist of even greater talent. The author of this magnificent collection had no desire to speak of himself and has entrusted me with this difficult task. I am sure that not even an entire volume would be enough to present the full range of his creations, ideas and his discretion, but essential activity towards the realization of many international masterpieces. This piece is only one tiny example: this condom-holder, rediscovered only recently in a drawer where ie had been left lying since 1970. At the time*

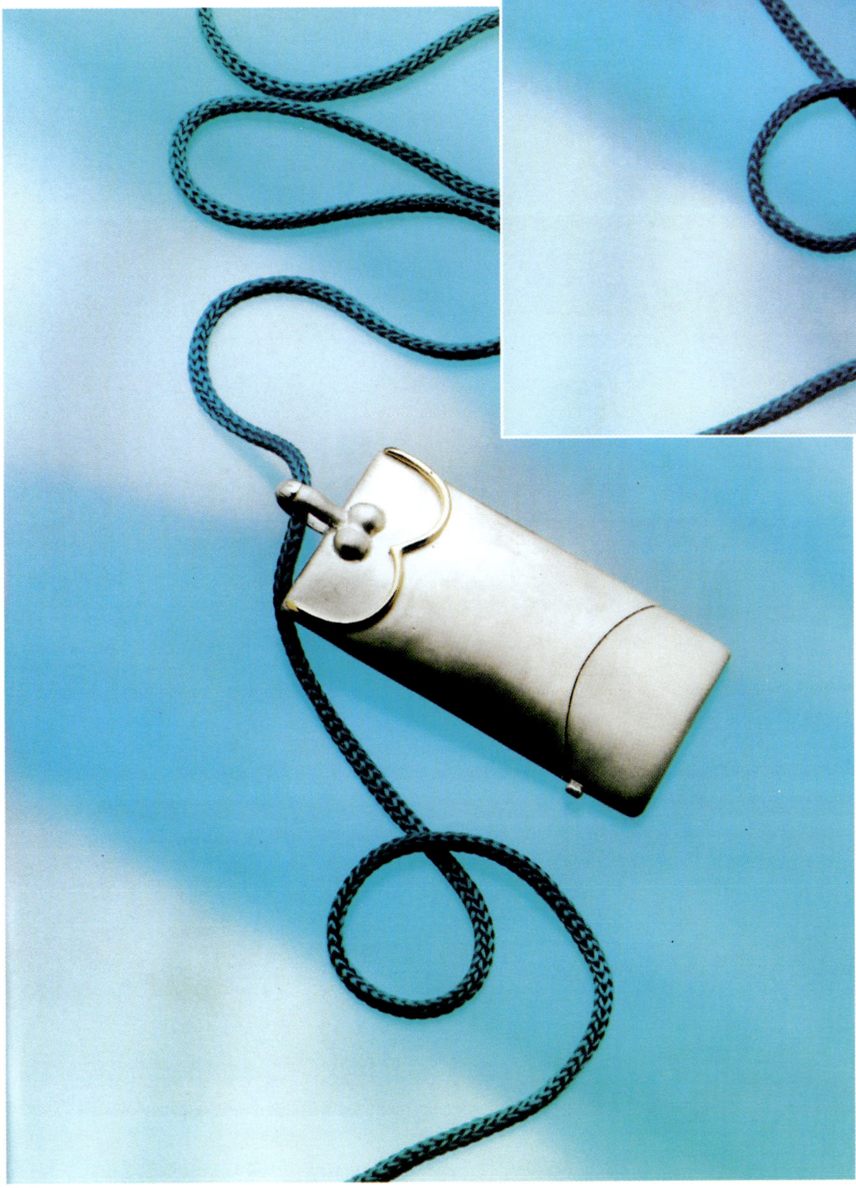

it was considered a useless object but for Claude Mazloum today it is an elegant way of demonstrating his active participation in the fight against AIDS. This jewel-object is a revelation, illustrative of its creator's foresightedness and points to his commitment. He takes care in transforming each object into a collection piece, without depriving it of either its usefulness or its reason for being.

François Renac, composer and passionate art lover, honorary doctorate in musicology.

DEBRA DEMBOWSKY, *"Love Goddess", brooch-sculpture in silver, mosaic, marble and alabaster*

VIVIAN PAUL ANTON, *vermeil wedding rings, called stefana in the orthodox tradition, hand-crafted using the most precious silver and decorated with pink and white freshwater pearls.*
In Greek orthodox nuptial ceremonies (as well as in other countries) the two rings united by a single link celebrate the union of husband and wife who become king and queen of their kingdom, as well as the union of man and God.
This tradition dates back to antiquity, when the nobles wore rings made of gold or leather and athletes were rewarded with crowns made from olive branches. The orthodox church has drawn on these practices, turning age-old traditions into modern symbols

CHAPTER XIII

Improvised Jewels

In collaboration with RANDA KHALIL

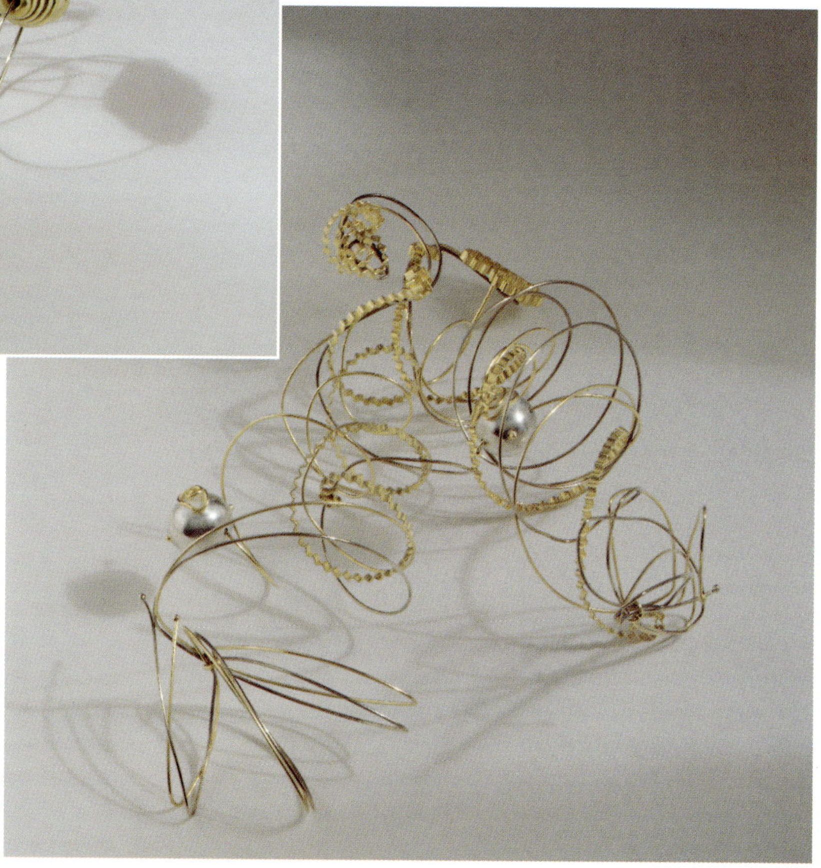

DESIGNERS OF THE 21st CENTURY

- WALID AKKAD
  41, Avenue Rapp – 75007 Paris
  41, Rue d'Athènes
  Achrafieh, Beirut/Lebanon
- TIZIANA and MASSIMO ALOISIO
  Via Malabranca, 1
  05018 Orvieto/Italy
- VIVIAN PAUL ANTON
  10822, W. National Ave.
  Milwaukee, Wisconsin/U.S.A.
- DANIELA BUFFAGNI
  Via Rua Freda, 8
  41100 Modena/Italy
- CAPUANO Jewelry Shop
  Via Veneto, 102 – 00187 Rome/Italy
  Nagai Bld., 1-7-7 Hacchyobori
  Chuo-ku – Tokyo/Japan
- ANNA CELLA
  Via Tortona, 68 – 20144 Milan/Italy
- WOO HYUN CHOI
  808-5 Yuk Sam
  Kang Nam – Seoul/South Korea
- CHRISTOPHE CLARET
  Manoir du Soleil d'Or
  2400 Le Locle/Switzerland
- CATHRINE CLARKE
  Rua Visconde de Piraja,
  547, Loja 110 Ipanema
  Rio de Janeiro CEP
  22415-900/Brazil
- DE GRISOGONO
  106/108 rue du Rhône
  1204 Geneva/Switzerland
- VIVIANE DEBBAS
  Centre Sofil, Achrafieh
  Beirut/Lebanon
- DEBRA DEMBOWSKI
  3212 S. 44th Street
  Milwaukee, Wisconsin/U.S.A.
- MARIA-GRAZIA DI GIANDOMENICO
  7, Via Alcide De Gasperi
  65025 Manopello Scalo (PE)/Italy
- EXTREME
  Mieke Govaerts and Tiziano Andorno
  Via Felice Cavallotti, 69
  15048 Valenza (AL)/Italy
- SIMONA FAVILLA and MARCO MINELLI
  Via Leopardi, 30
  00185 Rome/Italy
- FONDAZIONE PER LA PERLA
  Contrada Santa Croce, 14 C
  47031 Republic of San Marino
- CORNELIA FRECHE
  Angerstrasse, 4
  06118 Halle (Saale)/Germany
- ANDREA GALASSINI
  Viale Vicenza, 4/C
  15048 Valenza (AL)/Italy
- WILLIAM GERMANI
  Boite Postale 59
  Mansourieh/Lebanon
- MIRJAM GINSBERG
  Socinstrasse, 43
  4051 Basel/Switzerland
- ALBERTO GIORGI
  Corso Matteotti, 129
  61032 Fano (PS)/Italy
- DANIELLE GOFFA
  Gougbloemlaan, 7
  2980 Zoersel/Belgium
- CHRISTINE HAFERMALZ-WHEELER
  P. O. Box 105 282
  Auckland/New Zealand
- MELKON HAGOPIAN
  Centre Blanco – Beirut/Lebanon
- VINCENT JAUMIN
  38, Rue Joseph Wauters
  4802 Heusy/Belgium
- KEVORK'S Jewelry
  607, S. Hill St., Ste. 232
  Los Angeles CA 90014/U.S.A.
- KOALA PREZIOSI
  Via Del Fosso, 3
  52100 Arezzo/Italy
- Goldsmiths IL LEONE
  Via San Giovanni, 13
  50124 Florence/Italy
- SYLVIE LAMBERT
  Boite Postale 14
  16800 Soyaux/France
- ALICE HSIAO-YUAN LIN
  77-4 Chung Shan
  North Road, Section 2
  Taipei/Taiwan
- PHILLIP ERIC MAYNARD
  34, Hammer St.
  Christchurch 8001 – New Zealand
- CLAUDE MAZLOUM
  Schupstraat, 18/20 (boite 24)
  2018 Antwerpen/Belgium
- HUBERT MINNEBO
  Cathilleweg, 1
  8490 Jabbeke/Belgium
- MOUAWAD
  68, Rue du Rhône
  1204 Geneva/Switzerland
- BERND MUNSTEINER
  Wiesenstrasse, 10
  55758 Stipshausen/Germany
- SIMONNE MUYLAERT-HOFMAN
  Art galerie "La Reserve",
  Hotel La Reserve
  Elisabethlaan 160
  8300 Knokke-Heist/Belgium
- STEFAN PAULI
  Gerechligkeitsgasse, 13
  3011 Berne/Switzerland
- ERWIN PAULY
  Blumenstrasse, 39
  55758 Veitsrodt/Germany
- PERLES DE TAHITI
  Boite Postale 20470 – Papeete/Tahiti
- MARCELLO PIZZARI
  Via Cappelletta della Giustiniana, 24
  00123 Rome/Italy
- Diffusione PLATINO
  Largo Toscanini, 1 – 20122 Milan/Italy
- ANTOINE PREZIUSO
  28, Chemin des Raclerets
  1284 Chancy-Geneva/Switzerland
- ANTONINO RANDO
  Via Campofiori, 12
  24011 Almé (BG)/Italy
- LORENZO RICCI (RCM)
  Via Camurati, 45
  15048 Valenza (AL)/Italy
- DONATELLA RIGHI FORTUNA
  Piazza Capri, 1 – 00141 Rome/Italy
- ROBERGE
  68, Rue du Rhône
  1204 Geneva/Switzerland
- AGATHE SAINT-GIRONS
  49, Rue de Paris
  93100 Montreuil/France
- CHRISTOPHE SCHAFFO
  Chez Guenet
  2406 La Brévine/Switzerland
- KURT SCHAFFO
  Monts, 76
  2400 Le Locle/Switzerland
- HANS SCHINDLER
  Am Markt – 59494 Soest/Germany
- SEGI
  Haachtsebaan, 108
  3140 Keerbergen/Belgium
- JEAN-MARC SIEGL
  54, Rue d'Antibes – 06400
  Cannes/France
- KYRIAKOS SOMOS
  157, Route 303 – Valley Cottage,
  New York – NY 10989/U.S.A.
- THERESE SUDRE
  Avenue de France, 89
  59600 Maubeuge/France
- GREGOR TELGMANN
  Wesrstrasse, 41
  59174 Kamen/Germany
- NICK VAN DEN BRANDE
  Nachtegaalstraat, 44
  8800 Roeselare/Belgium
- KRISTA e GRETY VANDEVELDE
  Hoge Steenweg, 33
  1850 Grimbergen/Belgium
- BATIA WANG
  Artist Village
  30890 Ein-Hod/Israel
- GABRIELE WEINMANN
  et WIGBERT STAPFF
  Kapellenweg, 3
  69121 Heidelberg/Germany
- TEREZA XAVIER
  Rua Visconde De Piraja,
  351, Loja 213 Ipanema
  Rio de Janeiro CEP
  22410-003/Brazil
- ZARKHANE
  59, Achterstraat
  9270 Laarne/Belgium
- MICHAEL ZOBEL
  Rosegartenstrasse, 4
  78462 Konstanz/Germany
- ALBERTO ZORZI
  Via Malfattini, 17
  35010 Loreggia (PA)/Italy